I0709177

Jim in Tub

May 1976: auto-photograph by Jim Stewart
a "before" shot of 766 Clementina Street

Folsom Street Blues

A Memoir of 1970s SoMa and Leatherfolk in Gay San Francisco

Jim Stewart

Palm Drive Publishing®
San Francisco CA

All inquiries concerning performance, adaptation, or publication rights should be addressed to Publisher, Palm Drive Publishing, Publisher@PalmDrivePublishing.com. Correspondence may be sent to the same address. Send reviews, quotation clips, feature articles, and academic papers in hard copy, tear sheets, or electronic format for bibliographical inclusion on literary website and in actual archive.

Cover and interior design realized by Mark Hemry, Sebastopol, California

Published by Palm Drive Publishing, San Francisco CA
EMail: Publisher@PalmDrivePublishing.com

Library of Congress Catalog Card Number: 2011922848
Stewart, James 1942-
Folsom Street Blues:
A Memoir of 1970s SOMA and Leatherfolk in Gay San Francisco / James Stewart
p. cm.
ISBN 10 1-890834-03-3
ISBN 13 978-1-890834-03-6
1. American Literature—20th Century. 2. Masculinity. 3. Homosexuality. 4. Gay Studies. 5. Erotica—Gay. II. Title.

Printed in the United States of America
First Printing, July 2011
10 9 8 7 6 5 4 3 2 1

www.PalmDrivePublishing.com

To my partner, Ken Warner,
for all his patience in putting up with me
while I was writing of my past.

Acknowledgments

A very special thanks to Jack Fritscher
for all his encouragement, encyclopedic memory,
and suggestions in the writing of *Folsom Street Blues*.

To Mark Hemry for all his artistic
and technical expertise.

Foreword

Writing about the past is like exploring a photographer's darkroom. You never know what might develop. There is a time when secrets once kept in the dark must be brought to light. Now is the time to reveal them.

Unlike many gay archives that were secretly scrapped by embarrassed families or discarded by unsympathetic landlords, mine were cached in an old suitcase at the back of my closet for over a quarter century. The brown leather suitcase my folks gave me when I left home at 18 had morphed into a traveling repository inhabited by secret negatives, contact sheets and prints. From this archive, bolstered by 20 years as a research librarian, the recollections of friends, and current electronic data bases, I have developed the story of my life as a gay man in San Francisco's SoMa district in the 1970s. That place, at that time, is a necropolis I hope to resurrect with this memoir. Come, take a peek in my darkroom as I develop my story.

At the time, my life was part of the "secret" San Francisco some considered unsafe to enter, especially after dark. Graham Robb, in *Parisians: An Adventure History of Paris,* said of Napoleon III that "He might wonder how much of Paris he has really seen, and how anyone can be said to govern a city so full of secrets." San Francisco of the 1970s was full of secrets and half-secrets alluded to at A-list parties and in newspaper columns. Mayor George Moscone was said to wander the Tenderloin at night with his bodyguard pals, looking for secrets. In the end he too was unable to govern a city so full of secrets. It killed him.

A gay critical mass was reached in this "Baghdad by the Bay", as *San Francisco Chronicle* columnist Herb Caen called the City, between the Summer of Love in 1967, and the summer of 1982, when we realized gay pneumonia, gay cancer, and a number of other non-treatable diseases added up to AIDS.

Anthropological, political and medical papers, studies, theses, dissertations, and screeds have been written about gay San Francisco in the 1970s. They can be consulted for the study of gay movements and trends, collectives, statistics, politics, and theories. I've written how I recall myself as a gay man then, living my life as a fanatical moderate. I've written of others I knew then, too. Some show up in the papers and studies. Some don't. Others should be in the history books, but have been forgotten.

It was a time before political correctness, personal computers, and cell phones directed our lives. "The past is a foreign country," L. P. Hartley wrote in the prologue of *The Go-Between*. "They do things differently there."

San Francisco itself seemed a foreign country then. The things we did then were in the time and the place in which we lived. Like actors in film classics, we smoked cigarettes. We drank too much. We did drugs. We had unprotected sex because a quick trip to the V.D. clinic and a shot in the ass would take care of anything we might pick up. A joke at the time has the first man in a bar asking, "Where do I know you from? Do you work in a bank? It's somewhere I go all the time." The second man replies, "I work at the V.D. clinic."

It was a time and a life that crushed some. Many gay men took drugs, fucked until dawn, joked about the squalor they lived in, hung out on the street corner, and lost their youth. Some took their youth to the pawn shop, hoping to redeem it some day. Others buried their youth and we mourned. It was a time and a life that gave still others an inner strength that lasted a lifetime.

San Francisco in the 1970s drew men from across the United States, Canada, Mexico, Europe, Australia, and the world beyond. If you were a gay man and lived in San Francisco, the City, during that marvelous decade, you didn't need to travel. The world came to you. A drifter from Tulsa, Oklahoma, living in a single-occupancy hotel room, went home with a man from London who was living on trust funds from his family's diamond mines in Africa. A farmer's son from North Dakota crashed with the son of the president of Ford Motor Company Europe. When somebody asked you what you did, they didn't mean your job. They meant what were your sexual talents, your specialties, the fantasies you wanted to explore. Gay San Francisco of the 1970s was democracy's poster child. It was part of the gay migrant/immigrant experience.

The gay community within itself was segregated. There were three geographical areas that attracted gay men. There was the older gay quarter centered around Polk Street. Perhaps as an homage to gay Berlin between the World Wars, as depicted in Christopher Isherwood's *The Berlin Stories*, the street was fondly referred to as Polk Strasse. Others called it Polk Gulch. It catered to queens, gentlemen of a certain persuasion, some disco dollies. There were the all-American boys who flocked to 18th and Castro streets, the area called simply the Castro, or Castro Village, or the Village. And then there were leathermen and bad boys who gathered along Folsom Street, South of Market, the area that morphed into SoMa. Of course there was the Tenderloin and the Flagg Brothers shoe store on Market Street, where rough trade could be picked up. For a price. There were no hard and fast lines drawn. The whole City was fluid. The whole City, in fact the whole Bay Area, became our playground.

This is the story of men who worked with each other, and for each other. It tells of men who shared with each other. It recalls men who exchanged the art they had created, who told each other where the hot esoteric films were being screened. It paints a picture of men who picked up their tools and built playrooms in their homes and in their bars. The reader learns of men who exchanged ideas and partied together. And yes, it's a story of men who had sex together. In as many different ways as possible.

Some may ask if this is really how lives were lived then. It is. But not by everyone. I've written this account as creative nonfiction, literature's fourth genre. Some readers who did not live at that time, and in that place, may think this a work of fiction. There will be those who did live then and there, but have chosen to forget. There will be those who insist the Cordon Bleu restaurant never served Vietnamese Five-Spice Chicken, or that the Cento Cedar Cinema never screened *Salo.* So be it. Everything written here really happened. The dialogue approximates the original dialogue. The story is not linear, but represents the multifaceted lives lived at this specific time, in this specific place. It is a collection of anecdotes of gay life South of Market in the San Francisco of the 1970s.

It's my hope that *Folsom Street Blues* sheds light on a great experiment, one that made life an art form in that once upon a time City by the Bay. Those of us who lived in that San Francisco of the 1970s, like those who partook of *A Movable Feast* in Hemingway's Paris during the 1920s, find that wherever we go for the rest of our lives, that time and that place stay with us. All three components—time, place, and self—were essential parts of that whole, of that total experience. This is the story of that convergence, of my experience.

Contents

Foreword ix
The Flat on Clementina 1
Handball 15
The Trouble with Clarence 17
Smoke Signals 29
French Mussels 45
Man About Town 47
The Shapeshifter 59
Five Spice Chicken 79
Voodoo 89
Chasing Film 103
Beach Theater 119
The Naked Wine Thief 121
West Coast Beef 131
Bad Boy Art South of Market 133
Camille O'Grady as Muse 149
Up At The River 165
Mercedes Headed North on 101 179
Back from The River 185
Sweetbreads 201
Epilogue 203

Illustrations

Jim in Tub ii
Jim Stewart xvi
What a Dump 41
Johnny Gets His Hair Cut I 42
Johnny Gets His Hair Cut II 43
Jack Fritscher at the Slot 44
Keyhole Studios: Men South of Market 46
Bound Feet and Bound Hands 78
Luc at the Pacific Ocean 78
Jim Stewart – Photos 81
Leatherneck Bartender Ron 82
Leatherneck Poster 83
Spring — from the series Four Seasons of Ass 84
Summer — from the series Four Seasons of Ass 85
Fall — from the series Four Seasons of Ass 86
Winter — from the series Four Seasons of Ass 87
Max for Mr. CMC — 1978 88
Jim with Cigarette 118
Bill Essex 120
Keyhole Studios' Hot Stuff Etc. 132
Camille O'Grady Bell, Book, and Candle 148
Three Toilets 156
Malefactors with Bound Crucifix 156
Jim Stewart Photos at The Ambush 158
Camille O'Grady with Skull 159
Dancer David Studach 160
Daddy's Glove and Pistol 161
Drugs, Sex, and Leather 162
Putting on the Ritz: Top Hat and Blow 163
Robert Opel with Skull 164
Camille and Sybil 178
Jim Stewart – Photos: Town and Country 181
Lou Rudolph at Keyhole Studios on Clementina Street 182
Steve The Bartender: Drummer Compound 183

Geno The Greek 184
766 Clementina Street 202
Jim Stewart and Ken Warner 211
End — Clementina Street 213

Jim Stewart

1976: auto-photograph by Jim Stewart at Golden Gate Park

The Flat on Clementina

The fog crept off San Francisco Bay and into the warren of narrow streets in San Francisco's South of Market district. I glanced into the oversized rearview mirror outside the window of my pickup truck parked by the crumbling curb. "End Clementina" was reflected back at me from the corner street sign. I peered out the windshield. The building beckoned me from across the street. There it sat, shrouded in afternoon fog. Chunks of its cement-gray stucco façade had fallen away. It beckoned me like the gap-tooth grin of a two-bit hustler.

What a Dump.

When Bette Davis uttered her famous epithet in the 1949 film *Beyond the Forest,* she hadn't seen the flat I had just leased near Folsom Street, in San Francisco, California, U.S.A., on May 1, 1976.

The derelict structure I had bound myself to stood at 766 Clementina, an alley-like street one block north of Folsom, in a district of the City known as South of Market, South of the Slot—for the cable car slot that used to run down Market Street—or sometimes just Folsom.

South of Market in the 1970s was composed of various interlocking communities. There were pre-World War II rundown residential buildings usually composed of two or three flats. These low-rent, often absentee landlord buildings, lined the secondary alley-streets and were home to the Resident-People who lived there. Mom-and-pop corner grocery stores and cheap diners were scattered throughout this grid of grungy structures.

Rumor had it these streets were named for the Gold Rush good-time gals like Dore, Minna, and Natoma. It was an area that Baron Georges Eugene Haussmann, who directed the rebuilding of Paris during the 19th -century, would have razed.

Then there was a mixture of small light industrial businesses, such as a sandblasting machine shop, a scrap gold-and-silver recovery plant, or a redwood knickknack factory that wholesaled souvenirs to the National Parks. Most of these small businesses were located on the secondary alleys, some on major streets. Along the thoroughfares, such as Howard, Folsom, and Harrison, there were starting to be seen a few trendy to-the-trade outlets, featuring such items as display mannequins, industrial office furniture, or high-tech lighting. These were most often housed in former warehouses. They were interspersed with buildings that still were warehouses. Here worked the Day-People. Most left before dark.

Also along the thoroughfares, especially Folsom Street, were leather bars and bathhouses that catered to that sense of naughty danger sought by men who came into the district after dark. They were the Night-People. Threaded throughout this entire grid in both non-gentrified warehouse lofts and walk-up rundown flats were not-quite-yet-discovered-artists. They were mostly male and attracted to the masculine sense of blue-collar-place. And yes, they were also attracted to the cheap rent and the easy sex.

The place I leased was in an Edwardian-style post-earthquake/fire building. It was the entire top floor of a stacked two-flat. Sometime in the 1930s the outside had been resurfaced with cement stucco applied over chicken wire. By 1976 the chicken wire had lost a quarter of its stucco skin.

The flat had been vacated in a hurry. Piles of dirty clothes and discarded junk littered the seven rooms on the second floor. An old refrigerator was filled with rotting hamburger, rancid rice, and at least four generations of cockroaches. Windows were cracked and painted shut. Large chunks of plaster had fallen away revealing aging wooden lath. Both inside and out, the building looked abandoned. *What a dump!* I stared at the lease I had just signed for the top-floor flat: $150 a month. *What a steal!*

When I first moved to San Francisco, October 1, 1975, I lived with Jack Fritscher, a great friend, who had "sponsored" me to the City by introducing me to his circle of friends and the most interesting bars and bathhouses I could imagine. As a carpenter-in-residence, I turned his cellar into a bedroom and all-purpose playroom. On March 1, 1976, I moved into the Castro, San Francisco's expanding gay neighborhood. I shared an apartment on Noe Street with Sheldon Kovalski, an expat from Brooklyn, who had recently relocated up to San Francisco from Los Angeles. That apartment was within walking distance of 18th and Castro Streets. Sheldon soon left and moved in with a lover. I couldn't afford the place by myself. I had to be out by the end of the month. I wasn't sure where to look for another place.

In early April, 1976, I drove out to Lands End. It was a wild place then, out by the Pacific, southwest of the Golden Gate Bridge. It would later be tamed and developed as a National Recreation Area, but back in the day, it was visited mostly by adventurous men who went there for nude sunbathing and sex. Prides of once-domestic cats that had become inconvenient for their owners were dumped there to live free. It was a good place to watch the tides and think about life and the future or to contemplate which of the hot raw hunks on the beach there might follow you behind the rocks for a private session.

I had been wandering most of that afternoon on trails that were natural, carved out by hikers rather than the Parks and Recreation Department. The area seemed abandoned. Native vegetation reclaimed old cellars and foundations of long-demolished shacks. It could be dangerous there, what with the feral cats, wild men, and nude sunbathers. There were also predatory hustlers out for whatever they could get. I spent the afternoon admiring the wildlife, the Pacific, and wondering where I was going to live.

I returned to Merrie Way Road where I had parked my pickup. Before I reached the parking lot, I noticed an extremely muscular man wearing army pants and an army cap. It was the old-style cap, the kind that seemed to snap to attention and make you think of either the young Fidel Castro or the French Foreign Legion. Or both. Its shirtless wearer was pissing against a tree. I followed suit against a tree near his. He nodded acknowledgement of my presence and a smile broke his bearded face. His blue eyes joined his grin. I had just met Bill Essex.

After trading afternoon quickies in a nearby acacia copse, I followed Bill's mustard-yellow van to the Café Flore on Market Street. The café was near my soon-to-be-vacated apartment on

Noe Street. I had been by the funky place several times before but had never stopped there.

"You've been here before?" I asked Bill as we entered the café. It had the look of an elegantly scruffy greenhouse abandoned decades ago and only recently turned into a shabby chic café. Plants were everywhere. Ferns hanging from the ceiling competed with huge pots filled with rubber plants and ficus. Well-worn folding chairs and tiny tables that looked like immigrants from the cafés of Paris formed intricate patterns on the uneven floor through which waiters wound their way. Non-obtrusive disco music—was there ever such a thing?—could be felt as much as heard just above the din of diners.

"Yeah, I've been here before. A couple of years ago when they first opened," Bill said, as we waited for a table.

Seated, our drink and food orders taken, we entered the tentative world of conversation that often seems awkward after sex with a stranger.

"I'm looking for a place to live," I said. "I have to get out of my place up the street here at the end of the month. I don't suppose you know of any place that's cheap, do you?"

"As a matter of fact I do," Bill said. "A friend of mine, David Hurles, lives on Clementina Street. I sometimes stay with him when I come up from Pomona. He said there's been a For Rent sign on the place across the street for six weeks or better."

"Where's Clementina?"

"South of Market, near Folsom."

"What's it look like?"

"It's a dump. I don't know what the rent is but it can't be much the way the building looks."

"I want to see it. Is there a phone number to call?"

There was. Bill drove me over to Clementina Street after we finished at Café Flore. He was right. It was pretty run down. I copied down the landlord's name, Clarence, and his phone number. It wouldn't hurt to find out how much the rent was and what it looked like inside. Maybe inside it wasn't as bad as outside.

David Hurles' place was across the street. Bill Essex evidently had known him for some time. We went over and knocked. He was home. Hurles had just started a new mail-order photo and audio tape business, *Old Reliable.*

"I figured people will feel they can trust a place called *Old Reliable.* Don't you think it sounds like it has been around forever; that you wouldn't be ripped off by *Old Reliable*?" Hurles asked.

"I've never been ripped off by my old reliable," Bill Essex said.

We all laughed as Bill spread his legs and leaned back in his chair with his hands clasped behind his head so we could get a better view as his old reliable thickened in his army-surplus pants.

"How long have you been living here?" I said. "What's it like living in the Folsom area?"

"Jim's thinking of moving South of Market. He got the number for that place across the street," Bill said.

"I like it here. Chuck Arnett lives just above me, you know. I sometimes hear him. He's quite a sexual athlete."

Chuck Arnett worked at the Ambush, a bar on Harrison Street. Lean and quiet, in his 40s, he indeed had the look of a sexual athlete.

"So you feel safe here?" I pressed David. I had always felt safe visiting the bars and baths in the Folsom. The neighborhood here seemed quite different, however, than either Noe Street or 25th Street where I had lived with Jack Fritscher and David Sparrow.

"I feel as safe here as anywhere," David Hurles said. I caught a brief exchange of slight smiles between him and Bill Essex. Only later would I understand the significance of that exchange. David Hurles often picked up ex-cons and other marginal men for sex and photos. It was how he built *Old Reliable.*

That night Bill and I picked up where we had left off under the piss-trees out by Lands End. I had my first snort of cocaine. I took a series of photos of Bill in the shower. I concentrated on the superb musculature of his body. Although *Pumping Iron*, the bodybuilding photo book published a few years earlier, had been a hit with gay men, few gays at that time worked out and developed their bodies the way Bill did. I got a great shot of Bill emerging from the shower.

Despite his prematurely bald head and dark beard, with his college football-player body and broad infectious grin, he looked the epitome of the All-American Boy. In the background of the photo, hung over the toilet tank, was a framed picture of another

American icon, the Marlboro Man. In the morning, Bill left to return to Pomona, near Los Angeles, where he was working on a master's degree in landscape architecture at Cal Poly. Before the summer was over, Bill too had heard the siren call of the City and moved north to San Francisco.

Without realizing it, I had laid the foundations for my life as a photographer South of Market. I would move into the dump on Clementina. David Hurles would lend me an extensive mailing list for a photo mail-order business. And I had taken the first photos of Bill Essex. He would prove to be the top model for my Keyhole Studios mail-order business.

The first thing I wanted to do after leasing the flat on Clementina, before I moved in or took one load of garbage to the dump, was take pictures. They would function as "before" pictures in contrast to whatever "after" pictures I might take once I had rescued the place. They would not be *Architectural Digest*-style "before" pictures. I wanted the flat to first function as a dangerous-abandoned-wrong-side-of-the-tracks place, for suggestive blue-collar sexual fantasy photos. These first photos would be self-portraits. My only prop was a used yellow hardhat I found in a thrift store. The pictures would entice viewers to enter at their own risk. Don't try this at home. You can try it here, however. It was a personal performance piece. Pure theater. High-contrast black-and-white photos. It was the 1970s. It was *Art*.

The series included one of me, naked, wearing a hard hat, and sitting in an old clawfoot tub; Man Ray surrealism South of Market. Another photo in the series allowed the viewer to voyeuristically observe the naked hardhat exhibitionist through the narrow opening of a nearly closed door to a room filled with trash. I spent an entire Sunday afternoon in the flat by myself, setting up floodlights, positioning the tripod, and arranging the camera angles. I would focus on the spot where I would be, set the timer for the delayed shutter speed, then quickly pose for my own Nikon.

The afternoon sunlight, streaming through the streaked filth on the cracked windows, provided a new interpretation of the Venetian-blind-shadow-ladder-across-the-room technique, long a favorite of mine in the old *film noir* classics of the 1940s. It was

San Francisco South of Market. It was 1976.

When I finished I was exhausted. The creative energy I had put into the photo shoot had peaked in a total body climax. I packed my camera and equipment into the cab of the pickup truck, locked the door to the flat, and headed over to Harrison Street and the Ambush for a cold longneck beer and the camaraderie the place provided.

I got a beer at the bar and started up the stairway to the second floor. At the top of the stairs a man behind the counter in the leather shop looked up.

"Hi," I nodded as I rounded the landing and came up the last couple of steps.

"Hi." He nodded back.

"It smells good up here," I said.

"It's all the leather and poppers."

I laughed and inhaled deeply. "I'm Jim Stewart," I said, offering my hand. He had a firm grip. Just as I was letting go, his hand slowly collapsed into an elongated fist not much bigger around than the butt-end of a beer bottle.

"Chuck Arnett."

"I know," I said. "I'm moving into the place across the street from you on Clementina."

"I know," he countered with a shy grin.

My eyebrows arched in question marks.

"David Hurles."

This master artist of the leather scene, whose mural of manly men in the Toolbox bar had been published in the June 26, 1964, issue of *Life* magazine, when I was still an undergrad, smiled up at me revealing the whites of his eyes beneath their brown irises. Although in his late 40s, he still had the hard lean look of the dancer I'd heard he'd once been in New York. He wore a close-clipped mustache and chinstrap beard. His still-dark hair was cut short, military style. A longsleeved khaki shirt, worn Levis, and a black leather vest complemented his tight body. His sleeves were rolled to the elbow to display sinewy, nearly hairless forearms decorated with fading long-ago tattoos. His nails were clipped short.

As I watched, he finished a stylized ink doodle. It covered

the lower half of a cardboard back from a yellow legal tablet. The doodle was of a well-filled condom. He folded the cardboard in half and set it on the counter. Next to the drawing of the used rubber it read “Scum Bags Three for $1.00.”

“I like that sign,” I said. “Can I buy it?”

“It’s not for sale.”

He must have seen the disappointment in my eyes. He reached into the waste basket at the end of the counter and pulled out a cardstock ad for the Ambush. It had been printed with a script of the word Ambush and an Arnett drawing of leathermen’s heads. There was a whole stack of them next to the cash register. He laid it on the counter. I looked at it questioningly.

“Turn it over,” he said softly.

I turned it over. On the back of the card were preliminary doodles of several used rubbers, each slightly different. *Scum Bags* was drawn in a couple of different scripts. Arnett made a little mark in the corner that looked like some stylized zodiac sign.

“It’s yours,” he said as he slid it across the counter top toward me.

As I picked it up, I noticed a stain of some sort on the left side of the card. It spread across the drawings of the unrolled prophylactics. Probably spilled beer, I thought. I put it carefully in the inside pocket of my brown leather Harley jacket. I had just acquired my first original Chuck Arnett.

Removing the piles of dirty clothes, assorted junk and broken furniture that had been left behind in the Clementina flat was daunting. Thank God for heavy-duty yard waste bags and my pickup truck. There was a dump just out of the City in South San Francisco. Going there proved an adventure. Since I was not a professional trash hauler, most of the guys at the weigh-in station waved me through at no charge. My load looked light compared to the big-guy trash haulers and dumpsters that frequented the place.

As a bonus, I was directed to an area for household trash, not raw garbage. I love trash. What a treasure trove. Leftover building scrapes were often available. These went back to the flat for future use. One trip netted enough two-by-fours and two-by-sixes to build a small deck for potted plants in the lightwell off the middle room. Another time I found sheets of heavy plate glass. One was used as replacement glass for the original front entrance door. Another was sandblasted by a neighbor and used in a light table I built to view photo negatives.

Going to the dump was like going to the thrift store. Sometimes you hit paydirt, sometimes you didn't.

Finally the small trash was gone from the flat. The cockroach-infested refrigerator and grease-encrusted stove remained. Among the tools I had brought with me to California was a hand dolly for wheeling light loads. It would work fine for getting the appliances down the long flight of stairs. Once on the recessed porch, I could load them into the bed of the pickup. I strapped the refrigerator to the hand dolly with clothesline rope I had bought for a different purpose. The cockroaches and rotting food remained inside.

By fancy footwork I was able to get the bulky load out of the kitchen, down the hall, down two steps onto the landing, and started down the long flight of stairs. There were skids on the back of the dolly that would slide over the edge of the steps. I was halfway down when I heard the front door open. The mass of the refrigerator prevented me from seeing who it was.

"You need a hand there?"

"Yeah, thanks." Who the hell was that?

"I brought over some ceramic tile for the bathroom."

It was Clarence, the landlord. I wondered what sort of tile he brought for the bathroom floor. I pictured titty-pink squares with a gold scroll around the edge. He had said he would provide all the supplies for the renovation. A buddy of his was a building contractor with lots of leftovers. I would supply the labor. It was part of the deal. It was why my rent was only $150 a month.

"I can't see very well where I'm headed with this thing," I said. "Can you help me guide it toward the front door?"

I felt the old refrigerator shift slightly as Clarence gently guided it toward the door and out onto the recessed front porch. I let it pivot down as the weight slowly shifted until it was resting on the stoop.

"What are you going to do with it?" Clarence asked.

I wanted to say I'd leave it there on the stoop, in homage to junk that accumulates on front porches and along back roads across America. I thought better of it.

"My truck's parked right there, the GMC," I said, nodding toward Nelly Belle in front of us. "Since it's Saturday, and the street's not too busy, I think I can maneuver the truck crossways in the street. I can put the tailgate down, back up against the street steps, and load it right here from the stoop."

"That should work."

Thank God, I thought. Clarence wasn't going to give me a list of reasons why it wouldn't work.

"Want to give me a hand with the old stove?" I said.

He did. The stove was much lighter and easier to maneuver onto the stoop. I backed up the truck and we loaded the stove and refrigerator. I left Clarence to pull his maroon Ranchero into my parking spot. He said he would leave the boxes of tile for the bathroom upstairs. It proved easy pushing both the stove and refrigerator out of the pickup at the dump.

On the way back from the dump I debated with myself whether the tile would be like I first envisioned it, or maybe baby blue with a cluster of violets in the center. They were neither. They were French tiles, like the ones I had seen in the fleabag hotel I stayed at on the Isle St. Louis, in Paris, the summer I was 21. Their shape, of square-circle-triangle in chocolate, caramel, and cream, looked very *ancien régime*. They were perfect for the bathroom with the clawfooted tub. Maybe Clarence would be an easier landlord to work with than I had thought.

The transformation of the stage set had started; when finished, the flat would be changed from a dangerous-bad-side-of-town-abandoned-derelict-building to a mysterious personal performance space embracing sex, art, and the at-home salon. All would be secreted away, on a far-from-forlorn alley, in burgeoning SoMa, the South of Market district of San Francisco. It was 1976.

My stomach told me it was time for supper. It was almost dark. I was tired. A trip to the Norse Café in the Castro was out of the question. Then I remembered. It was Monday. The H. Salt Esq., a couple of blocks away on 7th Street near Howard, had a Monday night special. For 99¢ you got "authentic English fish and chips," complete with malt vinegar. True, they weren't wrapped in the *London Times* but for 99¢ they weren't bad.

I parked Nelly Belle just back from the little chain outlet, went in, and laid down my 99¢. I scooped up my two cod fillets and French fries, doused them with malt vinegar, went back outside, and hopped into my pickup for an English picnic. The overhead streetlight was burned out. That's probably why I noticed the candle burning in the top floor bay window of a rundown two-flat across the street. The flickering light was casting shadows. They were moving with a certain regularity, would stop and then start again. I stared long at the shape in the window. A man was jacking off in candlelight, by the bay window.

He stopped. I quickly turned the pickup's parking lights on, then off again. The masturbation continued. I unbuttoned my 501s and pulled out my cock. I paced my jerking rhythm to that in the candlelit window. It felt great. I wanted him to know how much he was appreciated. I turned on a small light on the dashboard and increased my pace. The phantom exhibitionist also increased his pace, to match mine. Voyeur and exhibitionist merged, became one. We each licked the warm sticky results from our hands for the benefit of the other. Not bad. Dinner and a show for 99¢.

I looked at my watch. It was 9:30 PM. I switched off the dashboard light and looked up at the bay window. The candle had been extinguished. The show was over. The following Monday I returned at 9:15 for the fish special. I also got a repeat participatory performance in the candlelit bay window. This continued for a month. Then I missed a Monday. The following Monday the window was dark.

Moving day was a bitch. The contents of my GMC covered wagon I had moved to California, a little over six months before, were scattered between two locations. Nearly half of my stuff I had left at Jack Fritscher's house on 25th Street. The rest was at my apartment near Castro, on Noe Street. The most important items to move, of course, were my camera and equipment and my carpenter's tools. They were the instruments of my livelihood.

My goods also included an assortment of mismatched mid-19th century walnut and cherry furniture, well-worn Middle Eastern tribal rugs, old theater spotlights, odd mirrors, modern paintings, a variety of old steamer trunks and ancestral pine primitive chests filled with frayed volumes of leather books, vintage photographs, and an assortment of woodland Indian baskets, salt-glazed stoneware jugs, as well as odd items of chipped china, tarnished silver, and pewter that pique one's interest when viewed in low light.

There was more. I had to move a collection of clothes that alluded to military men, lumberjacks, cowboys, jocks, farm boys, hardhats, and other blue-collar males. Then there were the leathers, including a couple of motorcycle jackets, chaps, leather pants, and vests. With all this was a hooded handwoven wool burnoose from my visit to Tangiers, my academic gown complete with hood striped with bright colored silks, a black Edwardian suit I bought in Paris, and other dapper duds. And of course my old Harris Tweed sports jacket.

There was also the mounted deer head of an eight-point buck my dad shot the fall I turned 13. I'm a collector. It was all grist for personal performance theater and photo shoots. It also led to some smoking-hot sex. It was art.

Jack Fritscher and his lover David Sparrow had offered to help me move. I planned the move on a Saturday, when Clementina Street was not as crowded. Saturday had been a good day to take the stove and refrigerator to the dump. I hoped it would be the same for the move. We loaded both my truck and Jack's Toyota for the trips from his place on 25th and Douglass and my former digs on Noe Street. All had gone well. We managed to find parking spaces where we needed them. The move was nearly finished.

"This is the last load from the truck," David said, as he brought an armload of clothes up the long stairway and into the middle room. He laid them across the old steamer trunk my great-Aunt Mae had left behind when she died at the state mental hospital during the height of the Great Depression.

"Did we get everything out of your Land Cruiser, Jack?"

"I think there's a couple of old used jockstraps left in the back if you want them."

We all laughed.

Jack Fritscher, my bridge to the leather world of San Francisco, had been carrying used jockstraps in his Toyota Land Cruiser since his days as a college professor. Whenever he offered someone a ride, Jack would wait for their reaction to the aroma. Some confused it with that new-car smell. Others were surprised they suddenly had secret thoughts of their high school football coach.

"Well, I guess that's it. Thanks for all your help," I said as I looked around the room piled high with my possessions.

"Well, don't we get the grand tour?" Jack said. "All we've seen so far is this room and the stairway."

"The best two rooms in the place," I joked half seriously. "Of course you get the grand tour." I walked over to the double pocket doors leading to the front parlor. I got one door open just over six inches when it refused to slide any further out of its pocket. The other door refused to budge at all. There was a nervous chuckle all around as Jack and David eyed each other.

"Well, I think that needs a little work," I said. "We can go in the other way." I led them into the hallway and back into the front parlor.

"That's a beautiful fireplace," Jack said.

"Isn't it?" I agreed. "It's amazing it has never been painted." It was indeed a handsome fireplace. The old oak surround still had the patina of its original finish. A beveled plate glass mirror, uncracked, was still mounted between two slender Doric oak columns above the mantel. All the tiny green glazed tiles surrounding the fire box were intact.

"Does that heater work?" David asked, pointing to an ancient enameled-metal gas burner from the 1940s that sat in front of the fireplace.

"I don't know, but it's going to the dump," I said.

"We don't want you asphyxiated," Jack said.

"I really like the French curve at the ceiling," I said. "Both this room and the middle room have it."

Jack and David cast their eyes upward. Nearly a quarter of the plaster from the ceiling was missing, revealing the old wooden lath underneath. The French curve was intact.

"And the bay windows," I continued, "they're in the front bedroom as well. Aren't they neat?"

We all looked toward the front bay windows. Frayed sash-weight cords dangled from all three units. The upper window on the right was cracked. Looking through the streaks left from dirt and rain, the bay windows revealed a panoramic view of overhead wires and several crossarms for both electric and phone wires. A round electrical transformer dominated the view out the cracked window.

"That's Chuck Arnett's place right across the street there," I added, as way of compensation.

And so the grand tour went. Neither Jack nor David seemed impressed with the well-worn 1950s linoleum in the kitchen that displayed grease outlines and rust circles where the stove and refrigerator had sat They left shortly afterward, but not before Jack had asked me quietly if I was sure I knew what I was doing here, and what sort of papers I had signed. I reminded him of the little workingman's Victorian I had restored back in Michigan. He hadn't seen the "before" scenes of that little beauty. It was comforting to know they had my best interests at heart. After they left, I locked up the place and headed for the Ambush. Had I really gotten in over my head? I kept thinking of the East Village roach-infested tenement I had stayed in over Thanksgiving during my last year as an undergrad. At least here the bathtub wasn't in the kitchen under a breadboard.

Boy, did I need a beer.

Handball

Sweet dew of night
Still nestles in Rhododendron Dell
While a multitude of Orphic birds as if
Conducted by
Seiji Ozawa
Welcome dawn into the park

Inconspicuous
You stand there
Tall and slender
Cleverly hidden
Tensed
As if before a pitch

Young mustached face
Seductive curve of
Corded bronze forearm
Strong delicate hand
Cupping the ball
Ready for action
All suggest
A night spent
South of Market

You
Swept silently through
The Slot
Last night
Mesmerizing all
Like you dominated
Parisian salons
A century ago

Luis Buñuel's young woman
In frustrated passions of
L'Age D'Or
Fellated marble toes
Of Apollo in the garden

Now many yearn for
Your bronze arm
Perpetually on display
In Golden Gate Park

The Trouble with Clarence

In the fall of 1975, I hauled ass along I-80, across the Great Plains, over the Rockies, and on into the City by the Bay. I got to cruise cowboys in Cheyenne and get it on with Mormon missionaries in Salt Lake City. Meanwhile, Clarence Thompson had closed a deal on a two-flat on Clementina. Clarence got the rundown dump South of Market in San Francisco for $24,000. Cash.

"Why cash?" I asked him.

"Well, the girl I bought it from, Elena Gonzales, said she wanted cash. I didn't have it sitting around, so I went to my bank. They gave me a loan for the $24,000. I gave it to her. Counted it out for her right there in the bank, all in one hundred dollar bills, at her request. She signed a quitclaim deed over to me. It wasn't until later I found out why she wanted cash."

I sensed a good story was coming. Clarence, I found out, was good at stories. He was a Minnesotan who married a Guatemalan beauty. Clarence's graying blond hair, which he wore combed straight back from his forehead, in the manner of men his age, and his pale blue eyes, gave him a Midwestern-Scandinavian look. He was not quite short and not quite fat and had passed the big five-oh.

Clarence lived in a 1950s ranch-style house out in the Sunset District, not far from the Pacific Ocean, with his wife, mother-in-law, and 16-year-old daughter. Like many straight men, he needed to get away from his womenfolk once in a while. He felt comfortable South of Market. It was a man's place.

"Why'd she want cash?"

"Well, what I didn't know at the time was she didn't really own the place."

"She didn't own the place! I thought you said she gave you a quitclaim deed."

"Oh, it was in her name, alright. Everything was legal. The

thing is, her brother thought he still owned the building. She sold it out from under him."

"How'd she do that?" I was warming to his story.

"Elena's brother, George Gonzales, bought the house on the GI Bill sometime after World War II. About 10 years ago he had a heart attack. He was afraid he wasn't going to make it. If he died, he knew the building would go to his wife. That was fine, but he feared her brother would somehow get it away from her. He hated his brother-in-law. He signed the house over to his mother, who was living with the sister here, in the upstairs flat." Clarence's arm swept out in a wide gesture to include the whole upstairs.

"So how did Elena get title to the place?" My head was starting to spin.

"Well, it seems the old lady, shortly before she died, signed it over to Elena so the son, George, couldn't kick his sister out. Elena had never married. The old lady thought she was looking out for her daughter."

"Looks like Elena was able to take care of herself, after all."

"Looks that way. The problem is, Gonzales still thinks of this as his place. He doesn't think he has to pay rent. Mrs. Gonzales told me what happened."

"What are you going to do about it, Clarence?"

"I told him he could stay here six months rent-free. After that I'd have to charge him."

"That's pretty generous. What'd he say?"

"Nothing. He just went back inside the flat. His wife nodded her head and followed him."

"It's not a language problem is it?"

Clarence laughed. "No. It's not a language problem. Elena told me they were Californios. They've been here since before the Gold Rush."

"Their six months must be about up, aren't they?"

"Two months ago."

"What are you going to do?"

"I'm not sure."

Clarence and I were standing in the kitchen surveying the empty room. Spraying Raid and laying down Combat traps had brought the cockroaches under control. For now. They were probably lurking elsewhere in the building, waiting to return as soon as the lights went out.

"How'd you happen to come across this place? Was it through a realtor?" I said.

"No, it was actually at an office party." He chuckled.

I knew more of the story was coming.

"Last Labor Day we had an office party out at that old beach house at the end of Golden Gate Park, near the Great Highway. The Beach Chalet."

"Isn't that the place that has some great WPA murals?"

"Yeah, there are old paintings on the walls. They might be from the 1930s."

I made a mental note to check out the place. WPA murals were part of Roosevelt's New Deal program and had always intrigued me. I wondered if these murals showed sailor boys in tight-assed bell bottoms the way Paul Cadmus' WPA murals do.

"Anyway," Clarence continued, "I was talking with Elena, just shooting the shit. She was a secretary at work. A nice girl. A good secretary. When I mentioned I was looking for some investment property, she asked if I wanted to buy her place."

"What'd she say about it?" I said, thinking of the mess it had been in.

"She just said her mother left it to her when she died, that she didn't want anything in her flat, she just wanted to walk away and leave with the 24 thou in cash. Walk away clean, as she put it. When I saw her apartment I knew why she just wanted to walk away. I would too. She was always neat at work, well-dressed. I never understood it. But boy, 24 thou is a steal, even if the place is a mess."

I nodded my head in agreement. "Is she still at work?"

"No, she split for L.A. as soon as she had the money. Never told her brother she had sold the place. Just up and left."

"Did she tell you anything about her brother?"

"No, she just said the first-floor flat was rented."

Clarence liked to surprise me. When I least expected it, he would show up with a load of salvaged supplies for the renovation of the flat. It was part of the deal, of course, but I had envisioned buying the supplies and giving him a receipt for reimbursement. Clarence had a friend who was a construction contractor. I think most of what he brought to the flat was leftovers from construction jobs. A lot of things were top quality. It was just his unannounced delivery system that made me jumpy.

The day I officially left the apartment on Noe Street and became a resident on Clementina Street was a jumpy day. Clarence's contractor buddy had installed new copper plumbing in my flat. He had lifted some of the floorboards in the kitchen, bathroom, and toilet room, cut notches in the joists to accommodate the new pipes, and then replaced the old tongue-and-groove boards.

I nailed down pressed-board subflooring over that tongue-and-groove in the bathroom in preparation for laying those great French floor tiles Clarence had brought over. The bathroom arrangement was very European. The stool was in a small room by itself, the toilet. The clawfoot tub and lavatory were in a larger separate room, the bath. Both were just across the hall from the back bedroom, The Other Room.

I took a break, had a cigarette and some Gatorade in the front parlor. It was hot. My shirt off, I stood in front of the open bay window, catching the afternoon breeze. The street was empty.

The faint smell of redwood sawdust and the low drone of a table saw drifted in from the shop next door. Across the street, in the open stairwell, I saw a man knocking on an apartment door. It was the building where Chuck Arnett and David Hurles both lived. There were four apartments in the building. All were accessed by the open stairwell in the center of the building. No one answered the door.

The man came back down the stairs. He was wearing faded Levi's and a plaid flannel shirt open halfway down his hairless chest. His sleeves were rolled up past his elbows to reveal well-developed biceps. There was a black leather thong tied around his neck. His dark hair was clipped short. He wore a mustache. He looked like he had found his way here from Castro Street.

He stepped out from between two parked cars next to the narrow sidewalk; looked in both ways up and down the street.

It was still empty. It was sunny, although a light wind had come up. He must have glimpsed me when I drew on my Marlboro and exhaled a stream of smoke out the window. The breeze carried my smoke across the street. He looked up. I smiled. He smiled back and rubbed his crotch suggestively. I did the same in the open window. He crossed the street. In a minute I heard my front door being slowly opened. Footsteps started up the long flight of wooden steps.

I was waiting for him at the top of the stairs. Neither of us said a word. I turned and nodded toward the open door to the small toilet room. He entered. The room wasn't much bigger than the pay stalls at the Greyhound Bus Station. He unbuttoned his beltless Levi's, took out his dick, and sat down on the toilet. There was just room for me to stand in front of him as he started to undo the metal buttons on my Levi 501s. Without a word we soon reached the rhythm and pitch brought by the thrill of danger that's the excitement of anonymous sex in a public toilet. But it wasn't a public toilet. It was my flat on Clementina. It was performance theater for two. It was Art.

I heard the entrance door at the bottom of the stairway open and someone step in. I shot my load to the thrill of being caught in *flagrante delicto*.

The sound of a heavy box being set on the bottom step was followed by retreating footsteps on the outside cement steps. The door had not been closed.

Without a word, I stepped out of the small room, closed the door, and buttoned my fly. I was waiting at the top of the stairs when Clarence reached the landing with a box of small blue and green glazed tiles.

"For the kitchen counters," he said, only slightly out of breath.

"In the back," I said, not offering to take the box. "There's something I want to show you on the back porch."

We walked past the closed door of the toilet and back to the kitchen. Clarence set the box on the floor. I led him out the back door onto the decrepit enclosed porch dominated by an old laundry sink.

"I think I can set the tile cutter up in this sink and fix up a hose for a fine water spray when I'm cutting tile."

He agreed. "I'm parked right out front. I need a hand with the tile cutter."

We headed down the hall toward the stairs. The door to the toilet was open. As we passed I glanced in. A large wad of cum floated in the old stool. The Castro Clone had also shot to the thrill of almost being caught.

I headed to Folsom Street for lunch at a place David Hurles told me about. It was run by young men with beards and shaved heads. Sounded hot to me. It was a noontime meditation meal. Your dollar donation brought silence and seconds of brown rice, tofu and tiger's milk.

When I walked in I saw at once how the saffron robes clung to the young men with the shaved heads. They were naked beneath all that gauzy orange. I knew I wasn't allowed to say anything. I sat down. A somewhat warm glass of tiger's milk was set in front of me. Had it just been milked from a tiger? An earthen bowl filled with dollar bills was passed around. I added my dollar to the collection. A plate with sticky brown rice and bean curd was set in front of me. Filling, but short on flavor. What the meal lacked in flavor was made up for by the sensuous movements of the naked men under the saffron robes. The usual kitchen smells were replaced by those of sandalwood and male sweat.

I returned several times for a noontime meditation meal. Then one day they were closed. I read in the *Bay Area Reporter*, a free gay newspaper, that it had all been a drug front. They had been busted.

I spent the remainder of day-one residency continuing to nail down the pressed subflooring in the bathroom. I mentally planned my order of attack on the place. The toilet was usable, though in need of a little work. I had just proved that. The kitchen was a large project. It would involve tearing out a wall shared with the dining room, installing new cabinets, tiling countertops and floors, and patching and painting old plaster walls. Dining at a variety of cheap restaurants in San Francisco in 1976 was not a deprivation. The kitchen could wait.

The bathroom involved tiling, restoration of the clawfoot tub, installing frosted glass in the window, jury-rigging a shower, and finding an old pedestal sink. The tiny corner lavatory was past restoration. In its place Clarence had left a baby-blue 1950s wall-mount porcelain monstrosity. The bathroom would take some time. It too could wait.

In the meantime I could wash up at the old laundry sink on the back porch. Showering at any of the bathhouses South of Market was a delightful depravity.

The room that would be given top priority, I decided, was the small front bedroom with the bay window. It was over the recessed front entrance. I could hear anyone coming or going from either flat. By completing it first, I would have a great getaway oasis. I could escape there from working on the mass disaster of the rest of the flat. It would also provide a civilized area in which to entertain, or repair to after more vigorous sessions in the wreck of the back bedroom, the room I thought of as The Other Room. Yes, the front bedroom would take top restoration priority.

As I washed up on the back porch, in the old laundry sink, I thought of the "whore's baths" I used to take in my sleazy room at a fleabag hotel on the Isle St. Louis in Paris the summer I was 21. Just the essentials. Face, pits, and crotch. I wiped my wet hands on dirty Levi's, pulled on a clean black T-shirt, and donned my brown leather Harley jacket. I was ready.

I did a walkthrough of the flat. The back door was locked, the windows closed. As I headed past the bathroom I noticed a small wet spot on the pressed subflooring I'd been nailing down. Must be I'd spilled my Gatorade. I was becoming addicted to the stuff.

I was lucky. I found a parking place for my truck on 18th Street in the small lot around the corner from Castro Street. The afternoon crowd was off the street. The night cruisers hadn't come out yet. Still I got "the look" and "the nod" from half a dozen or so hot men between my truck on 18th and the Norse Cove Café on Castro Street. I entered the domain of Dragon Lady, the mystery woman. Maybe she was French, and her name was Germaine. Maybe she was an Egyptian Jewess who inspired

Lawrence Durrell's *Justine*. Whoever she was, Dragon Lady, with her husband, ran the Norse Cove Café.

The food, Scandinavian and French bistro fare, was served cafeteria style. You went through the line, picked your entrée and sides, found a table, finished your meal, and paid at the counter. No waiters, no check. A great meal could be had for a buck. Dragon Lady was known to chase you down the street if you failed to pay. She saw all. She knew all.

"Jim!"

I looked around.

"Over here."

I saw Sheldon Kovalski eating by himself. I hadn't seen him since he had moved out of the apartment we shared on Noe Street, and in with his lover, John Ely. I went over to his table, squeezed his shoulder, and started to shake hands.

"Oh, give me a kiss. This is the Castro."

I did.

"How's your place on Clementina coming?" Sheldon hadn't seen it yet.

"Fine. Let me get some food and I'll tell you all about it."

I asked for a plate of *pommes a l'huile*. I added a smoked sausage and one of Boudin's sourdough rolls to the warm French potato salad. As I put Dijon mustard on the sausage, I noticed Dragon Lady watching me. She knew exactly what I was eating, what I was drinking. Black coffee.

"Where's John?"

"Out somewhere, having a good time, I suppose. So, you're all moved in?"

"Yes sir, I'm an official denizen of Folsom, as of today." I told him about the flat, sparing none of the gory details. Sheldon looked intrigued. He had grown up in Brooklyn and lived in Los Angeles for a number of years. LaLa Land he called it. We finished our meals and remembered to pay.

"You headed back to Folsom Street?"

"Yeah. Want a ride?"

"It's a little early but why not, as long as I got a free ride."

I looked at my watch. It was a quarter to nine. It was early.

"How about the Ambush?" I said as we got in my truck.

"That's pretty laid back this time of day."

There was a parking space right in front of the Ambush on Harrison Street. Sheldon bought me a beer. We talked for a while and then each wandered off as we ran into other friends who had begun to drift into the bar. After midnight I left, by myself, and drove over to Folsom Street. No parking spaces were left. I circled around onto Clementina. Lady Luck smiled on me. A space was waiting right in front of my flat.

I walked back to Folsom Street and Playland, a leather bar across the street from The Slot, that infamous bath-house where I'd had my head shaved by Sheldon a month before. For nearly a year Playland, named for the long-gone amusement park out near the ocean, had hibernated. Tonight it was awake.

A line of men, waiting to get in, led down the sidewalk from the open door. Music boomed out of the bar. At the door a shirtless man, wearing a leather body harness, crossed his huge arms over his barrel chest. When a man came out of the bar, he would let another one in. The men in line were hot. It would be worth the wait. I got in line.

Some stood in spotless leathers practicing their S&M, standing and modeling. Others were in Levi's well-worn in the crotch. A whiff of poppers drifted down the line as disco blasted out the open door. A fist holding its thumb over a small brown glass bottle was shoved near my nose.

"Here. Want some?"

I took the bottle of poppers and held it just under my mouth and inhaled the fumes deeply before doing the same under each nostril. I started to hand it back to Well-Worn Crotch in front of me.

"No. Pass it along. It's from the doorman. He doesn't want us to get bored and leave before we get inside."

The effect of poppers doesn't last long, but the rush can be intense. The rush hadn't peaked when I saw an apparition. A short man with full black beard was coming down the sidewalk. He was dressed in gypsy-hippie rags. His long robe and wide-brimmed hat were complemented by dozens of dangly necklaces and spangled bracelets. A skinheaded tambourine hung from a cord around his waist. His dirty feet were bare. A miniature collie, wearing a red bandanna around its neck, trotted on its little legs, attempting to keep up. As he neared us, he picked up the collie. His jewelry rattled. He leaned in toward me.

"Pot?" he whispered.

I shook my head.

"Hash?"

I shook my head again. He moved on down the line. Ahead, I saw someone pull bills from a wallet and hand them to Gypsy-Hippie man. My poppers rush was gone, but the little collie and its master were still there.

"Who is that?" I said to the man in front of me.

"That's Jesus Christ Satan."

"Who?"

"Jesus Christ Satan." He laughed. "He's sort of an urban legend around here. Rumor has it he used to be a lawyer in New York. I think he came here in the 60s," he said, as if that explained everything. "He goes all over selling his drugs. The cops just leave him alone."

"Is he homeless?"

"I don't think so. I heard he declared his apartment's independence from the United States and applied to the U.N. for aid to developing nations."

"Nice if you can get it," the man behind me said.

We all laughed.

We were nearing the door. The music was louder. I saw Jesus Christ Satan cross Folsom Street. He had put the collie down again and it was working its tiny legs in a frenzy to keep up. They headed for The Slot.

Once inside I saw it was well worth the wait. The crowd, half-naked, swayed to the beat of throbbing and pounding music. The DJ built the pulse as the closing hour of 2:00 a.m. approached. By then, many of the sweat-drenched men would be gone, heading for the baths or home, having peaked during the mass orgy of sucking and fucking in the back room. The back rooms were what could make or break a bar in the Folsom.

I fought my way through the mass of bodies, groping and being groped, until I reached the bar for a cold one. With beer in hand, I headed for the back room.

The smell of booze and cigarettes, weed and poppers, sweat and testosterone, enhanced the dark scene of men moaning and grunting like rutting pigs. Soon I was part of the critical mass of male flesh, grinding its way to the ecstasy of Revelations. I was. I am. I am to come. I came. My body sang.

The din of disco music stopped.

"Repent, you motherfuckers, repent!" The metallic sound of a shaken tambourine could be heard above the grunting and moaning in the otherwise silent back room. Again. "Repent, you motherfuckers! Repent!"

Silence.

"We're not *mother*fuckers. We're *father*fuckers!" a deep voice from the dark bellowed out in passion.

A small dog barked.

Oh God, Jesus Christ Satan, I thought.

"Last call, gentlemen. Last call. You have ten minutes to drink up. It's time, please."

The lights slowly began to brighten. Most men stumbled out the exits and toward the baths. It was Saturday night, South of Market, San Francisco, 1976.

I headed back to the flat, threading my way in the dark down 8th Street and along the narrow alley-like confines of Clementina Street. Fog hung in a soft halo around the one dim streetlight that was still lit. An alley feline, searching in the remains of someone's supper, tipped over a galvanized garbage can, sending its lid rolling and clattering into the gutter as the cat ran across my path. Silence again.

My engineer boots on the concrete rang out in the early morning stillness. I made my way along the narrow sidewalk with its dark tunnels of unlit doorways. I stopped. I thought I heard footsteps behind me. Silence. I proceeded again toward my flat. Again I heard footsteps behind me. I stopped again, my heart beating, as if in sympathy with its earlier popper rush. Nothing. Then I heard a fountain splashing. I laughed. Some late night reveler, like me, had stepped into a darkened doorway to piss.

I reached the flat. My recessed stoop and steps were dark. A faint light found its way through the filthy glass in the old paneled door of my downstairs neighbor. It was close to three in the morning.

My first night in my new place. Why was I jumpy? I managed to fit the key in the lock. I entered and closed the door behind me. I locked it. I reached the top of the long wooden staircase in the dark. I found the light switch in the hall and pressed it. A 40-watt bulb, at the end of a braided cloth-covered cord extending down from the ceiling, came on. I stepped into the toilet room, took a long beer-piss, and flushed the toilet. The tank did not fill up. Great.

Bam! Bam! Bam! Someone was pounding on my front door. The short hair on the back of my neck bristled. Who the hell was knocking on my door at nearly three in the morning? I was no longer jumpy. I was pissed. I thudded down the long stairway, unlocked the door, and flung it open.

"What the hell do you want?" I bellowed.

A middle-aged woman with gray unkempt hair and wearing a worn-out chenille bathrobe, a relic of the 1940s, was standing in front of me.

"I'm sorry to bother you. My husband and I live downstairs and water started dripping through our bathroom ceiling. You weren't home and we didn't know what to do. We called Mr. Thompson. My husband said he could shut the water off in the basement so Mr. Thompson wouldn't have to drive all the way over here. So that's why you don't have any water."

"Oh." Before I could introduce myself or apologize for yelling at her, she slipped back into her apartment.

I went back upstairs. At least that explained why the toilet tank didn't fill up after I flushed. I checked in the bathroom. What I thought was spilled Gatorade when I left, had turned into a wet circular stain on the new subflooring I had nailed down that afternoon. I had nailed into the new copper pipes that were laid high in the floor joists. Clarence would be over tomorrow. I'd have some explanation by then.

I striped and lay on the thrift store mattress I had thrown on the floor in The Other Room. The odor of male sex still clung to my naked body. I'm going to like it here, I thought. I slept.

Smoke Signals

Smoke. Down on my knees laying carpet, I smelled smoke. I glanced toward the bay window facing the street. The small glass ashtray on the window sill held two cold cigarette butts. No smoke there. Outside it was sunny. This was unusual for San Francisco. By 2:30 in the afternoon fog would generally start to drift in from the Pacific. A slight breeze would pick up.

I went back to stretching the carpeting across the floor, hooking it onto the carpet tack-strips nailed around the edge of the room. I had never laid carpet before, but knew it couldn't be too difficult. I had done the reverse; ripped it up.

The carpet was sage green and textured like moss with no visible signs of wear. It had been taken from a much larger room in a much finer house out in The Avenues. Clarence, the landlord, said it had been a bargain.

The hard part of the bargain had been cutting it to match the irregular outline of the floor. This outline included a bay window, a fireplace, a light well, and several doorways. I was starting to get the hang of it: cutting, stretching, hooking.

The smell of smoke was stronger.

I glanced toward the bay window again. It looked like fog had started to come in. It smelled like smoke. I got off my knees and stood up. Bet I have carpet burns, I thought as I went to the bay window and pulled down the top sash on the left. I stuck my head out. To the east the street was shrouded in smoke. I couldn't tell where the fire was. The distant sound of sirens came closer.

I grabbed my camera bag from the kitchen table and slung it over my shoulder. I retrieved my bank books from the oak desk I'd trucked over the Rockies. The truck with my carpenter tools inside was parked on the street.

I double-timed down the inside stairs, closed the door and ran across the street to where Bill Essex lived. Smoke still hid the street to the east.

Bill and I had lived together, briefly, after he moved up from U.C. Pomona, where he was working on a master's degree in landscape architecture. He, along with Jack Fritscher, had applied for positions as deputies under the gay outreach program of Sheriff Richard Hongisto. Bill was waiting to hear on the status of his application. He had moved into David Hurles' old apartment across the street.

"Bill," I shouted through his door as I pounded on it. "Bill!"

I fumbled on my key ring for his apartment key. We had each other's keys for just such situations. I found it. I unlocked his door. He was sleeping naked on his king-sized bed. Bill pumped iron. I looked down at his body in repose. A scattering of hair covered the defined pecs and washboard belly Bill had worked so hard to develop. He was covered with a fine film of sleep-sweat. I had shot photos of that body in the woods in Marin County. They were hanging in the Ambush now, as part of my first show there, "Men South of Market." Later they were published in *Drummer*, the mag that Jack Fritscher, as the San Francisco editor-in-chief, turned into the 20th-century icon of the leather community.

"Bill, wake up," I shouted as I shook him.

Bill woke up.

"What the hell..."

"Do you know what you want to save?" I said.

"What the hell are you talking about?" he mumbled as he pulled a pair of army surplus fatigues up over his naked butt and wrestled into a white wife-beater shirt.

You could smell the smoke through Bill's closed windows. He pulled on his combat boots and we went onto the outside stair landing that ran through the middle of the building. We stuck our heads out past the railing to look down the street. The smoke was really thick now. Sirens sounded much louder. They were at the other end of the street.

Just as we looked to the east, we heard an explosion, and flames shot a couple of stories into the air.

"Holy shit!" Bill hollered. "What the hell was that?"

"Don't know," I said. "Could be that brick warehouse at the end of the street."

The afternoon breeze from the Pacific had finally made its way down Clementina Street and was pushing the smoke back in the direction it had come. It was fanning the flames at the end of the street. Fire trucks pulled up below us as we looked down from the second floor landing. No possibility of moving either my truck or Bill's van at this point. We raced down his stairs and up mine and into my bedroom where the bay windows hung out over the sidewalk and provided the best view.

The smoke had cleared as the flames shot straight up through what was left of the roof. Bill and I looked down and saw the sidewalks lined with neighbors. There was Enchanted Mary, the New Mexican artist across the street whose husband had left her for the proverbial younger woman. Chuck Arnett, who lived in Bill's building, was on the stair landing. The sleeves of Arnett's khaki Marine shirt were rolled past his elbows. His right forearm, with the aging tattoo, was slick with a thin film of white grease. Crisco? The hot young Hispanic from El Paso, who had moved into the building, came out and stood next to Arnett. He was barefoot and shirtless.

The widow in her 60s, who lived in the upstairs apartment next to the woodworking shop, was also out on the street. I watched her for a few minutes. She was dressed in a padded-shoulder pale green gown, with suede slingback heels: Joan Crawford come-fuck-me pumps. Right out of the 1940s. What an odd outfit to wear to a Saturday afternoon fire. But then again, one saw all sorts of fantasies played out here, on the streets South of Market. As I watched I noticed she would drift off the sidewalk and into the street. A young fireman would gently take her by the arm and say, "You'll have to step back on the sidewalk, ma'am." A few minutes latter she would drift out into the street again, where another young fireman would likewise pay attention to her. Who wouldn't love to play that game?

Through the center of the street, long hoses snaked their way toward the fire. Water, spraying from the hasty couplings at the fire hydrant, soaked the legs of the curious as they tried to get through the crowd. Firemen were everywhere, their protective clothing and helmets doing little to mask their strength and fitness. From our vantage point, Bill and I could easily pick out the bosses from the muscle. There were those who shouted orders and those who carried them out. All seemed to have mustaches.

A city cop car now blocked the end of the street. "Go home," I heard one young cop, also wearing a mustache, tell a group of the curious. "You can see more on the news tonight than you can here."

I looked toward the west end of the street. A mobile TV news truck was parked just behind the cop car. The field reporter, with his mike in hand, was backing his way through the crowd to take best advantage of the flames as a background. His cameraman was trying to keep up with him. He seemed more interested in filming the firemen and cops than the reporter with the flames behind him. It would make great footage on KPIX-Channel 5's news tonight.

I sat at the counter in Hamburger Mary's on Folsom Street eating chili. I liked the way it was served. A gob of grated cheddar on top would melt and run down among the beans. It was then thatched with a fistful of chopped raw onions. A full basket of saltines sat on the side. With a mug of black coffee my supper was under a buck.

I had walked the few blocks here since my truck was still boxed in by fire engines. The last of the big hoses were being rolled up when I left. The dark funkiness of Hamburger Mary's provided a hangout for all: men, women, straights, Folsom Street Daddies, Castro Street Boys, Polk Street Queens, hippies, and artists of all sorts who were trickling into this bargain-basement section of the City, South of Market.

Two guys in well-worn tweed sports jackets and faded Levi's sat next to me at the counter, discussing the fire.

"That wasn't much of a fire today, in the whole scheme of things," the one with the full beard said.

"You're right," the one with the clipped mustache agreed. "This whole area burned during the 1906 Earthquake," Mustache informed whoever wanted to listen.

"It was actually the fire that did more damage than the earthquake," Full Beard added.

"There was a bathhouse that burned right near here, at 10th and Howard, I think."

"Yeah, the James Lick Baths," Full Beard chuckled.

"I don't think it was that kind of bathhouse, not in 1906."

"Don't be so sure of it," Full Beard insisted.

Grad students in philosophy? Assistant profs of history, slumming from Berkeley? I finished my chili and headed over to the Ambush on Harrison.

Like Hamburger Mary's, the Ambush was funky. It was a cross between a hippie hangout and a leather/western bar. It was a beer-and-wine bar. It was not, however, a *wine* bar. Wine at the Ambush came from two jugs, red and white. You wanted rosé, they'd mix it right there for you. In the afternoon and early evening it was laid-back cool. Joints were shared. The heavy cruising mode wouldn't kick in until after midnight.

The Ambush was still in laid-back mode. I ordered a beer at the bar and headed for the meat rack.

"That was some fire today," the guy next to me said as he sucked on a joint and passed it my way. I shook my head.

"No thanks," I said with a slightly suggestive smile. "It's early yet."

"Whatever." He passed the joint over to the guy on his left, who greedily inhaled. Both were lean and lanky, sported dark wavy hair, sparse patchy beards, and needed a shower.

"Nothing like that fire a few months ago over on Valencia and 16th though," he continued. "Now that was one hell of a fire."

He inhaled his doobie and perfunctorily offered it to me again. I gave a little shake to my head. Grass had never done much for me other than make me sleepy. As it turned out, I was saving myself for a more magnificent obsession.

"That's where the Gartland burned, wasn't it?" I said.

I was sure of it, but wanted to hear his take on it. The Gartland Apartments, several stories high, had been a glorified single-occupancy hotel. It was filled with the near-homeless, addicts, artists, prostitutes of both sexes, as well as the general poor, and those on fixed incomes. It was also filled with city building code violations. The city had condemned the building and filed a lawsuit against the owner. In December, 1975, someone had poured gasoline down its main stairway and lit it. At least 14 people had died. Within days the building was razed before a full investigation could be launched. The hole in the ground where it had stood for over 60 years became known as the Gartland Pit.

"Damn tootin' it was," he said, "and me and him nearly burned up with it." He nodded toward the younger guy sitting next to him who had inhaled so greedily on the joint.

Now here was a story.

They hadn't been in the City long. Unlike me, they traveled light. They knew no one here when they arrived from Tulsa via Greyhound, sharing a single suitcase. They bunked at the Gartland with a man from Memphis they met at the bus station urinals. He gave up and moved back to Tennessee. They stayed on at the Gartland. No deposit required. The old hotel stood midway between Castro and Folsom. It was an ideal location.

"We was both sleeping. Man, had we partied," the boyish-looking pothead said as he grinned at me.

"Yeah, we woke up to the sound of sirens. There was smoke in our room."

"Never heard no fire alarm or nothing," Pothead Boy told me. "We thought we was cooked," he added, grinning at his own joke.

"What happened?" I urged them on.

"Well," the keeper of the joint went on, "the fire ladders wouldn't reach up to the top floor where we was. There was flames right below us. That damn floor was a-gettin' hot. We had the windows up, and looked down. There was a whole bunch of them firemen standing down there holdin' one of those big round jump things. Somebody was on a bullhorn hollering something but we couldn't understand it. Everybody was a-lookin' up at us."

There was a pause as they shared the joint again.

"So what happened?" I said.

"Well, we'd rolled this big joint when we first smelled smoke, so we just finished that doobie and got out on the window ledge and jumped. What a trip!"

"Yeah, we was holding hands when we jumped." There was a pause. "Hope that wasn't on TV back in Tulsa."

"Who gives a shit?"

"You guys want another beer?"

"We might," Joint-Keeper said, with the slightest of nods to Pothead Boy.

I headed over to the bar for beers.

After a few more rounds from my wallet, we walked over to Clementina Street and The Other Room.

"Man, did we party!" as Pothead Boy liked to say. I learned they were uncle and nephew and had been partying together since puberty.

In the morning they were gone. I had a hangover and an empty wallet. Had I really bought that many rounds at the Ambush last night or merely helped them stay in the City for awhile longer?

It'd been a month since the Clementina Street fire. Vehicles were still being ticketed if you didn't move them before the parking Gestapo arrived. I finally finished laying the used carpeting. It looked great. There was one more room in the flat to recover from decades of neglect. It was The Other Room. Bill had heard from the County Sheriff's Department. They wanted to interview him at his home. That was still listed officially as my place. I told him I would disappear during his interview the following week.

I locked the door and descended the six steps to the sidewalk. I was headed to lunch at Canary Island, a bright yellow streetcar diner over on Harrison with great burgers and dogs. I heard a siren. It was the braying of a fire truck warning all out of its way. I inhaled deeply. No obvious smoke. I looked east down the street. Already a crowd of neighbors had started to gather.

A thin trail of smoke was coming from an open second-story window a couple of buildings away. It was the upstairs apartment next to the woodworking shop. The widow-who-liked-firemen lived there. The fire truck nudged its way down the narrow street and stopped in front of the widow's building.

A handsome young fireman rode the truck ladder up to the open second-floor window. The thin trail of smoke had almost stopped. The widow, in pale pink negligee and peignoir, was leaning out the window. Her long gray hair hung around her shoulders in a style Hepburn would have been proud of before the Big War.

"Fire, fire," the widow was repeating. "Help me, oh please

help me," she said in a barely audible voice to the hot young fireman on the ladder.

He helped the lady in distress out the window and into his arms. She clung around his neck as the ladder was lowered. She was passed off to another fireman.

The widow promptly, and very properly, swooned against her rescuer and slide down his body toward the sidewalk where she sat leaning against his big rubber boots. She was crying softly. The neighbors, who had all gathered on the sidewalk, started to applaud. Was it for the firemen's heroism or the widow's great performance?

"Oh, for heaven's sake," someone whispered in my ear. "Have you ever seen anything so ridiculous?"

I turned. It was Enchanted Mary from New Mexico. The fire was now out. The hero was descending the ladder with the culprit, a metal wastepaper basket filled with charred newspapers. A pair of partially burned barkcloth drapes had been ripped from their rod and flung to the sidewalk below where they were quickly extinguished.

"You know her husband was a fireman?" somebody said, as much to herself as to anybody in particular.

I turned. It was Mrs. Gonzales, the woman who still lived in the flat below me.

"No," I said. "I didn't know that."

"Yeah." Mrs. Gonzales paused. "He was killed in a fire." Another pause. "They said it was arson."

"When was that?" I asked her.

"A few years after we moved here." She thought for a moment. "We both got our houses here about the same time. Her husband and mine both had the G.I. Bill so it must have been 1946 or 1947. No, it was probably 1948."

"She never remarried?" I asked.

"No," she said. "The house was paid off. She rented out the first floor and kept to herself. She's never been quite the same since then, you know."

I hadn't known.

Clementina was abuzz again. This time it was real Hollywood. Complete with movie stars. Or at least *a* movie star. Raymond Burr. The star of the early TV courtroom drama *Perry Mason* was filming a hopefully comeback TV series, *Kingston: Confidential*, on our street. Burr now played an investigative reporter out to solve crime. The crime on Clementina he hoped to solve? The burned-out warehouse fire at the end of the street. It was a perfect location. A real burned-out building, an industrial neighborhood in San Francisco, and lots of locals as extras.

The street was blocked off at both ends. Temporary signs posted the night before warned residents that their vehicles would be towed after 7 a.m. This was serious stuff, not just the whim of the parking Gestapo. This was Hollywood.

About mid-block a white van, with a stylized globe sandwiched between "Universal City" and "Studios" on its door, sat squarely in the middle of the street. Near it were several canvas folding chairs. "Raymond Burr" was boldly printed on the back of one. A handsome 20-something gaffer sat in it, tinkering with an electrical gang-box. Further down the street Raymond Burr, in a three-piece suit and top coat, was signing autographs.

It wasn't the Hollywood crew that caught my eye but a tall bearded local man. When he walked, you knew he was naked under his grease-stained dark blue jumpsuit. Dark chest hair curled out of it at his neck. A dirty white paper facemask rode high on his head, where a black watchman's cap barely contained unruly hair. The oval name badge sewn over his heart read Joe. I had seen him before on the street. He worked at the sandblasting place.

Big black rubber-encased electrical cables snaked down the street from portable generators, imitating the fire hoses of a few months ago. Two motorcycle cops, sporting the seven-point star on their gas tanks, were parked crosswise at the end of the street. One cop stood nearby, in his black leather jacket with SFPD emblazoned on its sleeves. His white helmet, with the same emblem, was pulled snugly over his head, its padded chinstrap dangling down suggestively. He wore a bemused smile beneath his smartly clipped blond mustache.

"Local lady!" a bearded guy in a faded blue golf jacket with *Rich Man Poor Man* printed on its back called out. "We're ready for the local lady!"

Two bag ladies, their handled shopping bags brimming with stuff, rushed forward. They both wore several layers of clothing. One had a faded scarf tied over her head. The other wore a green knit cap pulled down over her ears.

"Which of you's the local lady?" Bearded Guy said.

"I am," they both said at once.

"No, she's not," Faded Scarf said.

"She just came over here this morning because she heard you'd be here," Knit Cap said.

"No, I didn't. I'm here all the time. This is my street."

"No, it's not. She's crazy. She doesn't even know where she is."

"Whore!" Faded Scarf said, as she pulled the green watch-cap off the other's head, threw it to the ground, and spit on it.

The motorcycle cop with a neatly trimmed steel-gray mustache started toward the two women. Before he reached them, a man with overly stylized long hair, wearing a billowing white silk shirt with faded tight Levi's, stepped up to the ladies. He quickly took two 20s from his wallet and gave one to each local lady. The matter was quickly resolved by the Hollywood Fixer.

I walked over to Hamburger Mary's for lunch. The place was packed. I ordered a bleu-cheeseburger with sprouts and swiveled my counter stool around to people-watch. Hamburger Mary's was always a good place for people watching. Two women surrounded by tattered, overflowing shopping bags at a nearby table caught my eye. One wore a headscarf, the other had a green knit cap pulled down over her ears. Both were drinking drafts and wolfing minestrone as they chortled in glee at putting one over on the Hollywood Fixer.

I wondered if they were from the homeless colony that had sprung up underground between Mission and Howard. A square block had been razed in preparation for a new convention center. The huge hole sat waiting for the project to start. It would be years before the Moscone Convention Center was built there.

Along the north side of the hole, on Mission Street, were a number of underground rooms. They were the kind of rooms glimpsed through purple glass circles in the concrete as you scurried along the sidewalk. These underground rooms always intrigued me, but generally housed nothing more mysterious than a barber shop. With their buildings gone, they stood as an urban version of ancient pueblo cliff dwellings. Homeless people had moved in, organized, and elected their own mayor. I could picture these ladies as members of an ad hoc board of supervisors.

I often ran into homeless people South of Market. One day, before Hollywood came to Clementina Street, I went into a small blue-collar bistro on the corner of 8th Street and Natoma. It was in one of those old stores where the corner of the building was cut off at an angle with a double entrance door. Both doors were wide open that day.

I took the small table closest to the doors, in order to catch whatever breeze might be headed that way. You paid at the serving counter and went back for seconds. The diners were mostly workmen in sweaty clothes. I fit right in. I had steel-toed work boots, torn Levi's and a green work shirt with a red and white name tag sewn above of the chest pocket. "Jimmy" it read.

The special of the day was all the fried chicken you could eat. I had settled into my fried chicken, mashed potatoes, and canned peas when I sensed someone standing close by. There were no waiters but maybe it was someone I knew.

"Yimmy."

I looked up.

"Yimmy," a whispered voice said, "give me your chicken." An ancient-looking but once handsome man, probably no more than 40, stood in the doorway next to my table. "You can get more." I hesitated. "It's all you can eat," he said. He gave me a faint smile filled with bad teeth and swollen gums. He was still outside on the steps.

"Get out of here. I told you not to come in here again." The irate owner of the bistro pointed his finger outside and repeated "Out!" My newfound friend left.

I went back for a third helping of chicken. I carefully wrapped it in paper napkins when the owner's back was turned. I slid it inside the *Chronicle* I carried as a lunch companion and left it on the sidewalk a few feet around the corner. I headed for my pickup. By the time I pulled Nelly Belle into the flow of traffic, the chicken and newspaper were gone.

Walking back to Clementina Street from Hamburger Mary's, I was stopped by the Don't Walk sign at 9th and Folsom. There was another pedestrian waiting for the light. It was Raymond Burr. We stood there in silence for a moment. Just before the light changed he nodded at me. Maybe he would invite me to his private island in the South Pacific. Would I go?

"Know of any good bars around here?"

I waved my hand down Folsom Street. "Almost anywhere down this street for the next couple of blocks you'll see leather bars," I said. "Or if you want something more mellow, walk over a block to the Ambush on Harrison." I gave him directions to the Ambush. When the light changed he turned and headed for the Ambush.

The Gartland Pit at the corner of 16th and Valencia remained as a monument to eviction by arson. The sub-sidewalk Colony of Cliff Dwellers between Mission and Howard continued to demonstrate the tenacity of the homeless.

Bill Essex was accepted as an openly gay deputy sheriff. I now had a handsome set of photos of a genuine, naked, San Francisco County Deputy Sheriff.

Early one evening I heard a knock on my door. I left it unlocked most of the time. "Come in," I hollered down. "It's open." The door opened. I head heavy boots on the stairs. I came out of the kitchen just as the sandblaster in the grease-stained jumpsuit reached the stair landing. "Want a beer?" I said.

What a Dump

May 1976: auto-photograph by Jim Stewart,
a "before" shot of 766 Clementina Street

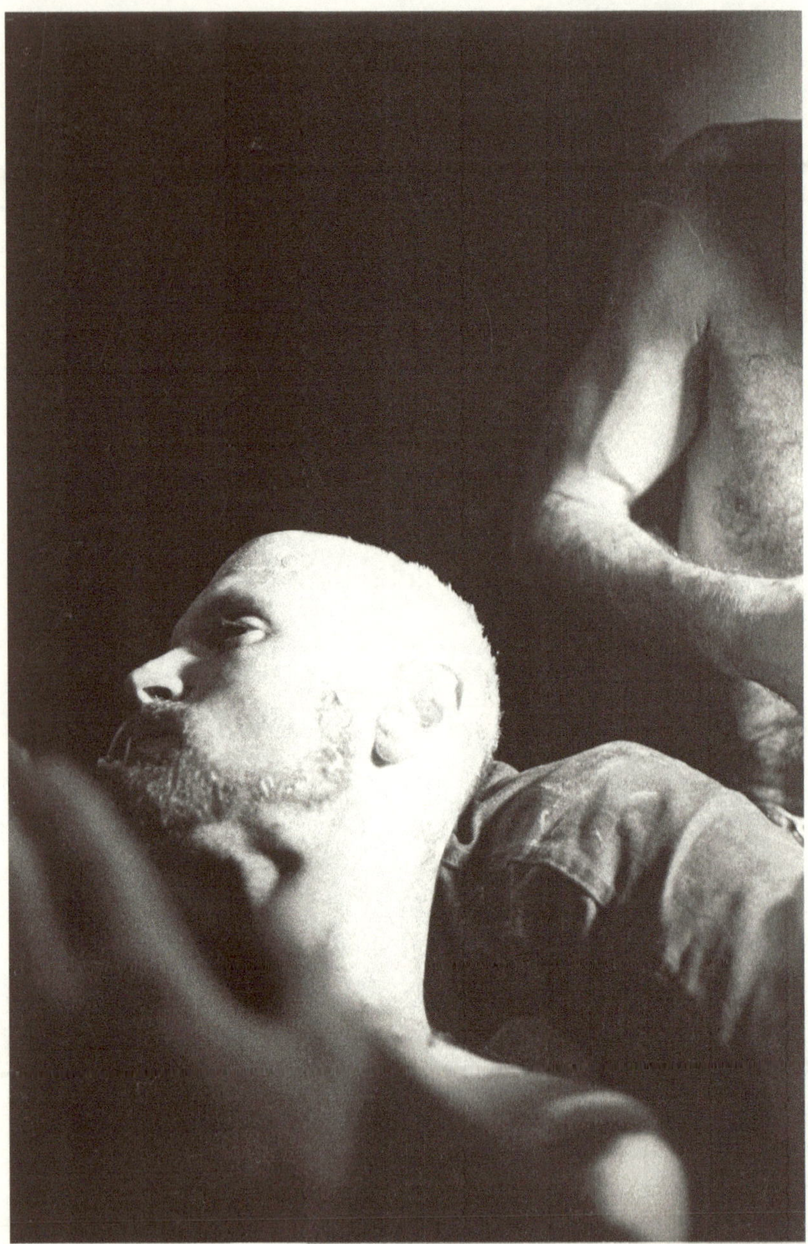

Johnny Gets His Hair Cut I

1976: photo by Jim Stewart at the Slot Hotel, 979 Folsom Street

Johnny Gets His Hair Cut II

1976: photo by Jim Stewart at the Slot Hotel, 979 Folsom Street

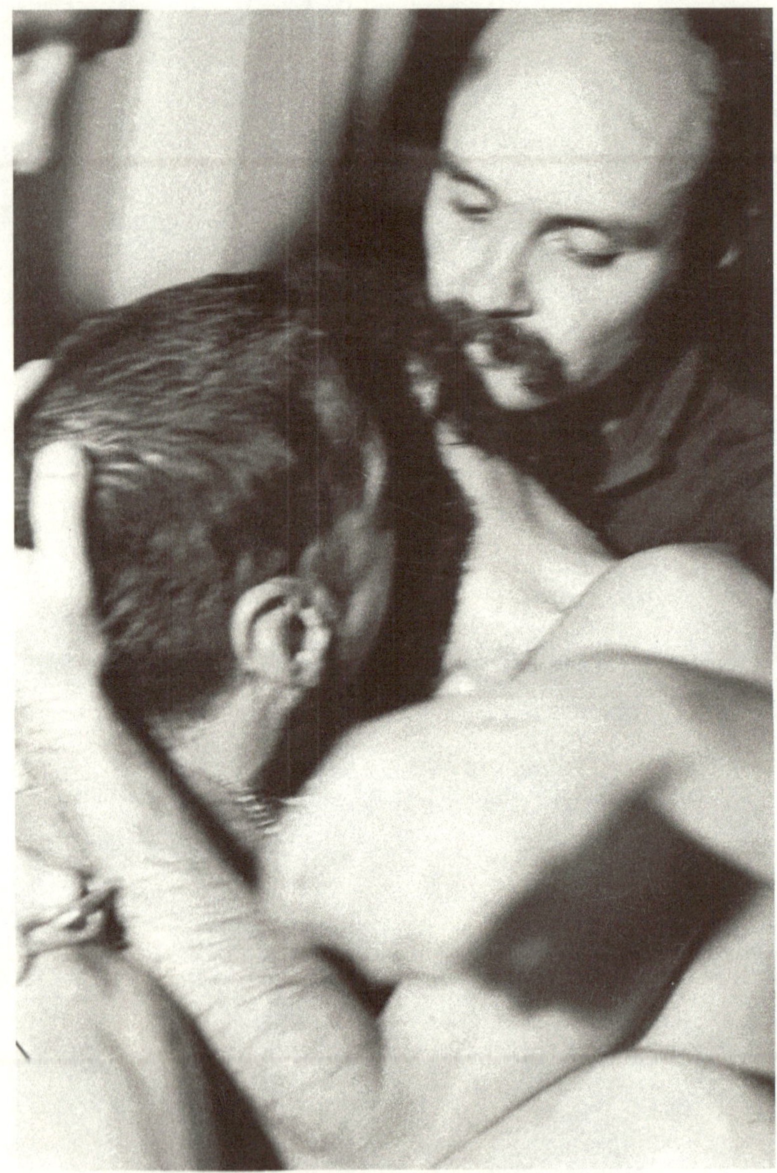

Jack Fritscher at the Slot

1976: photo by Jim Stewart shot at the Slot Hotel, 979 Folsom St. for *Drummer* (No. 16, 1977) feature "Johnny Gets His Hair Cut."

French Mussels

She ran away
With a fireman
In a Volkswagen van
Red and tan
California Gypsy-girl

He lived South-of-Market then
Shot high-contrast black-and-white photos
For group shows
In small side-street galleries
And wore black leather with white silk shirts
From Hong Kong

She and her fireman came
For a late meal
Of mussels from a market on 24th Street
Steamed in white wine with butter and thyme

The mussels opened
Revealing the soft double-lipped
Peach-hued bivalve within
Rimmed with dark flesh
Like an outline drawn by a soft brown pencil
Making an exclamation point

In the morning they were gone
Leaving only a lingering taste
Of briny mussels
And sweet white wine

KEYHOLE STUDIOS'

MEN
SOUTH OF
MARKET

PHOTOS BY
JIM STEWART

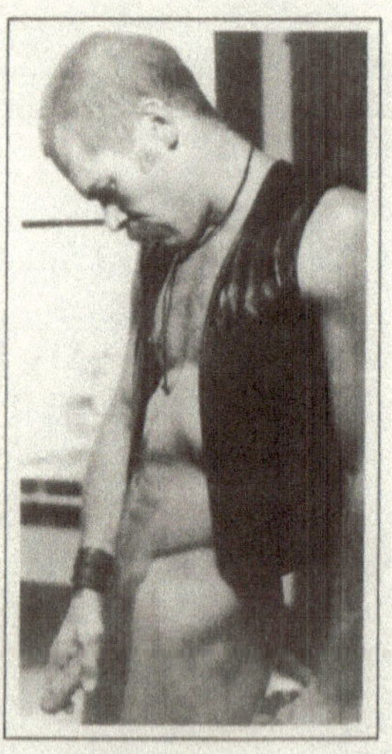

Keyhole Studios: Men South of Market
Photos by Jim Stewart

1977: model Michael Monroe, announcement for photo show at the Ambush Bar, 1351 Harrison St.

Man About Town

My first photo show had been hung in San Francisco. It was South of Market at the Ambush, a leather/western bar at Harrison Street and Dore Alley. The Ambush actively promoted the work of gay artists in the leather community.

The announcement for my show was a folded handout. The outside carried a drawing by Chuck Arnett of four hot leathermen. It read *Now at the Ambush.* Inside was a full frontal photo of Mike Monroe I had taken at my flat on Clementina Alley. He wore an open leather vest and a cock ring. That's all. It was one of the best-selling photos for my mail-order business. The copy read "Keyhole Studios' Men South of Market: Photos by Jim Stewart."

I saw red "sold" dots on a few of my framed photos. Although the announcement featured the photo of Mike, the hits of the show were the photos of Bill Essex. I had taken them during a private outdoor session in Marin County the summer before.

I was hanging out at the Ambush, posing ever so nonchalantly on the meat rack, hoping to look cool and disinterested and hot and available all at once. The meat racks were made for that purpose.

David Delay, one of the owners of the Ambush, had designed them. They were made of raw two-by-fours polished by hot male ass. Their width, height, and placement of the boot rail were all designed to store two-high stacks of longneck beer cases. The tops of the meat racks were like decking. Narrow spacing between the two-by-fours helped drain off spilled beer. They were a design marvel, faultless. They were soon copied in bars across South of Market and beyond.

Their height was great for posing. Anyone on their knees in front of you would find their face right in your crotch. You could lean back against the meat racks, thrust out what you had to display, and look hot. You could sit on top of them, hike your boots up on the boot rail, spread your legs, and look cool. A lot of thought had gone into their design.

"What do you think of the photos?" a man with a short, well trimmed chinstrap beard said. He wore a leather-n-wool letter jacket.

"Interesting," I said casually. He looked a little past the age to be wearing a preppy varsity jacket. He wore it well. I thought of locker-room jocks, the maturing coach. The Ambush welcomed a variety of fantasies, not just leather. We both looked at my photos. His eyes lingered on the naked Bill Essex, first as baseball player displaying his cock along the length of his bat, then as helmeted football player, airing his balls, after the game. Did he know I was the photographer?

"Where did you take them?" he asked.

"Up by Mount Tam," I said, "down a little two-track and up over a hill. I'm not sure if I could even find it again." I knew right where the turnoff was on the way to Mount Tamalpais, but I wasn't sure where this conversation was headed. Was he about to suggest that the two of us have a similar photo session there?

As it turned out, our conversation that Saturday night headed back to my flat. We had exchanged names and decided on my place on Clementina, a few blocks away. Tom slid his British-racing-green MG in behind my GMC pickup truck as we pulled in front of the building. We had been lucky with parking.

Upstairs in my flat we went right to The Other Room. We explored the sweaty world of locker-room jocks, using the very sports-fetish equipment from my photos.

Tom had tattoos. A lot of small non-related tattoos. Most guys I knew with tattoos were discreet. Jack Fritscher had a bull's head tattooed on his upper arm that hid behind a T-shirt sleeve. David Sparrow's stylized Scottish lion was similarly placed. The centerpiece of Tom's tattoos was a crawling black panther clawing its way down his left triceps, leaving behind red blood drops. It had been clawing Tom's arm for close to 20 years. Long enough to turn the black panther gray. Decorating the rest of his arm were tattoos bad boys give themselves in high school detention halls with ballpoint pens. Or later in prison. It would take a longsleeved shirt buttoned at the wrist to hide them. These tats did not belong to the Japanese school of aesthetics. They had not been done by Cliff Raven, the great tattoo artist from Chicago.

At dawn we took Tom's MG to Castro and a bar that opened at 6 a.m. on Sunday mornings. It was packed. Tom introduced me to dozens of men and the salty dog, a greyhound of vodka and grapefruit juice, with a rim of salt. He stuck with tequila sunrises.

Tom called Tuesday.

"I know it's really late, but I have an extra ticket for the symphony tonight." Pause. "Seiji Ozawa is back from Boston and will be conducting tonight." Pause. "Can I pick you up around 7:30?"

"Yeah, that sounds great." I looked at my watch. It was nearly 6:20.

"Don't worry what to wear. It's Tuesday, so it's skirt and sweater night." Pause. "I'll see you at 7:30. I'll just honk and you can come down."

The phone went dead.

Skirt and sweater night? I got out my all-purpose Harris Tweed jacket, clean Levi's, and a blue chambray shirt with a black knit tie. The tie I bought years ago at a flea market in Florence, Italy, for a couple of lire. It went with anything, could live forever in your jacket pocket, and never looked wrinkled. I had been wearing variations of this ensemble to events that required a jacket and tie for at least a decade. I could still get away with it.

At 7:25, I heard the muffled vroom of a sports car down on Clementina Alley, followed by the foreign honk of its horn. I was off to my first night at the San Francisco Symphony. Who the hell is Seiji Ozawa, I wondered.

Tom pulled the MG into a reserved parking space behind the War Memorial Opera House. The Louise M. Davies Symphony Hall would not open for another three years. A prominent sign stated "Reserved for Civic Center Staff Only: Violators Will Be Towed." I looked at Tom and raised an eyebrow questioningly.

"Aren't you worried you might be towed?" I asked.

"I know my way around," he said, as he gave me a lopsided

grin. The parking lot light reflected a faint gleam of gold in his mouth. The night was beautiful. We walked to a back door and entered the Opera House.

I discovered who Seiji Ozawa was. Not only did he have his own unique conducting style, he also championed modern classical music. Ozawa wore a white turtleneck with his swallowtails, rather than waistcoat and white tie. It was San Francisco. It was the 1970s.

Tom was right. He knew his way around. In his 40s, he was the quintessential man-about-town. His light brown hair was worn in what was once called a Kennedy Cut, after the President and his brothers. The ghosts of smiles past crinkled around his brown eyes. Tom was what once was classed as an "eligible bachelor." North of Market Street, he was Boston-Lace-Curtain-Irish, a son of Harvard. South of Market Street, Tom was Chicago-Southside-Irish, alumnus of the school of hard knocks. There were tattoos to prove it. He was a native San Franciscan.

A pair of season tickets to almost anything lived in his pocket. I would often get a call on the spur of the moment offering a "spare" ticket to the symphony. Sometimes I was sorely in need of sleep when Tom would call. One night I dozed off during the soothing sounds of the symphony. A slight poke awakened me. During intermission Tom gave me his lopsided grin.

"I give good symphony elbow," he said.

He never told me who usually used the extra ticket. Tom did mention a recent breakup with a longtime lover and a custody battle over the cleaning lady. Had he also won a custody battle over the season tickets? Or did Tom have a "culture buddy" who sometimes couldn't make it? An allusion to escorting single society women of various ages to events also slipped out. I never found out who the primary second ticket holder was. In fact I never found out much about Tom-the-Boulevardier. It didn't matter. The mystery was part of his charm.

My left ear had been pierced by Jack Fritscher when I was visiting him in San Francisco, before I migrated west. It was July 14th, Bastille Day, 1975. I was waiting to be picked up at Jack's place on 25th Street by a sailor from Mobile, Alabama, who I had met a couple of nights before at the Barracks, a hot and heavy bathhouse on Folsom Street. The sailor was going to drive me to the airport for my flight home.

"Are you coming back?" Jack asked, as I waited for the sailor to arrive.

"Yes," I said without hesitation. I had already made up my mind to move back to San Francisco. A decade earlier I had lived in the City the summer after I finished my undergrad work at Michigan State. It was time to return.

"When?" Jack said.

"The end of the summer."

"You're sure?"

"I swear."

"We need to seal that oath."

"Pierce my ear," I said in a flash. I had seen several guys in San Francisco with pierced ears. It was long before the big piercing craze hit the country. "Just leave a thread in it."

"I can do better than that. I have a fine gold wire. It's a nipple ring. It's my gift to you, so you'll return."

I sat on a chair in Jack's kitchen while he held a cork behind my earlobe and pierced it with a darning needle. With great patience on both our parts, he inserted the tiny gold wire hoop through the piercing. The hoop was about the size of my little fingernail. We had just finished when the sailor arrived and drove me down to SFO and my flight home.

The piercing worked. I returned to San Francisco in the fall of 1975. The small gold nipple ring in my ear had been replaced by a gold stud, half of a pair I had shared with Sheldon Kovalski when he moved up from L.A. and we lived together on Noe Street. That passion had not lasted long. We remained friends. He shaved my head one night at the Slot, that infamous bathhouse on Folsom Street. I kept the gold stud in my ear and the nipple ring in a black plastic film canister. It was now time to do something with the nipple ring. Tom was the man to do it.

With great ritual we prepared for my piercing. It was a rite of passage. Like urban satyrs, we were nearly naked, wearing only black leather chaps and steel cock rings. Tom brought a bottle of Korbel Brut. We entered The Other Room. It was lit by dozens of votive candles that drew dancing Picasso-shadow-gods on walls and ceiling.

A special audio tape compiled by Max Morales lent low mystic chords of music, like sea sounds in a cave. We alternated the champagne with lines of cocaine, laid out on an antique ivory mirror. All was enhanced with poppers, amyl nitrite. The ceremony spanned the night. During that hour that belongs to neither yesterday nor tomorrow, I received the gold ring in my left nipple. I was South of Market. It was San Francisco, 1977.

One afternoon, when Tom called, it wasn't to see if I could join him for an evening at the symphony. This time it was opera. I had been to an opera. Once. When I was 21, I saw Verdi's *Aida* at the ancient Baths of Caracalla in Rome. A team of four horses had galloped onto the stage pulling a chariot and a nearly naked charioteer. An elephant, leading a procession of young Roman soldiers, had followed. I didn't remember who the singers were, but for 49 cents worth of lira it was hard to beat.

"Do you like opera?" Tom asked on the phone.

I told him of my one experience.

"You'll like tonight, then. It's Massenet's *Thaïs* with Beverly Sills. We'll have dinner first. Pick you up 5:30-ish." The phone went dead. I brushed off my Harris Tweed jacket.

Tom was running late. The Thursday night rush hour traffic had been heavy. Fog had settled over South of Market, bringing a fine mist. I was thankful for the wool jacket as I waited at the corner of 9th and Clementina for Tom's MG. When it finally pulled up I jumped in and Tom took off with that British vroom as we headed north. The traffic had started to thin. We raced to Jackson Square and pulled up in front of Ernie's Restaurant on Montgomery, near the edge of the Financial District. We scrambled out as a uniformed valet appeared.

Inside I felt as if we had stepped back to the days of the

Barbary Coast. Massive mahogany pieces with beveled mirrors, stained glass, red walls hung with gilt-framed oils, and mounted game heads all lent the place a Victorian-bordello gentlemen's-club atmosphere. It somehow seemed familiar. I was sure I had never been here before. We walked to the black velvet ropes, where the maître d' stood in all his forbidding formal arrogance. Tom approached. The maître d' consulted his reservations list.

"Chop-chop. Opera night," Tom told him as he glanced around the room to see who might be there.

A barely perceptible nod brought a waiter to lead us to a table. I saw Tom nodding to several men already seated. He was smiling his lopsided grin all the way to our table. Tom, that devil, was showing me off.

"Does this place look familiar?" Tom asked.

"Yes, but I don't know why. I've never been here before."

"Did you see Hitchcock's *Vertigo*?"

Of course. Another, more famous, Jimmy Stewart had once dined here.

We opened with lobster bisque. Next came Kentucky limestone lettuce. Our final course was Normandy scallops with apples and Calvados. All was à la carte. Tom's treat. Dessert came after the opera. My treat.

We made it to the War Memorial before the lights dimmed. Beverly Sills, as Thaïs, beat *Aida* at the Baths of Caracalla, hands down. It hadn't even cost me 49 cents. Tom had some pictures he'd taken of Sills the last time she had been in San Francisco. He wanted to show them to her. To my amazement, we were allowed backstage, right into her dressing room. It was small. It was packed. Voices were jumbled, all talking at once. Bouquets of roses lay everywhere. Only one bouquet had found its way to a vase.

There was an energy-high in the room. It was not from drugs, but the energy from *Thaïs*, and especially the energy from Beverly Sills. She effervesced. Tom showed her the pictures, then laid them on her dressing table. He held her hand as he introduced me to her. Then he kissed her hand and we backed out of the room as more fans entered to worship the diva. I felt like a little stage-door Johnny in her presence.

Some time later, I heard an interview with Beverly Sills on TV. There was talk of filming *Thaïs*. The host of the talk show thought Sills would be perfect for the film.

"You've got to be kidding," Beverly said. "When *Thaïs* opens she's only a teenage girl. Do you know how old I am?"

"Well," the host continued, nonplussed, "it, uh, it could always be filmed through cheesecloth."

"Cheesecloth!" Beverly laughed. "Linoleum would be more like it!"

We left the War Memorial Opera House and made the rounds of a few bars. Instead of returning to my place on Clementina Alley, we drove to Tom's place. I had never been there before. He owned a two-flat near Cow Hollow on Green Street. He rented out the top flat. There was a two-car garage under the building. When we entered the flat, it seemed smaller than mine on Clementina. Its subtle elegance was writ large. The traditional tones of cream and gray, the fine Federal-style furniture, and the not-quite-cutting-edge mid-20th century art, all mirrored a setting from Woody Allen's *Interiors*. What caught my eye was a camelback couch upholstered in pale yellow-on-yellow silk stripe. We didn't linger there.

Tom confessed to scatological fantasies. There was a book out at the time, *End Product: The First Taboo*. It was the history of shit. For my birthday Luc had sent me a copy from New York. I was always interested in history and society's taboos. I loaned it to Tom. He was intrigued and wanted to explore that frontier. Some journeys beyond the Pale are enlightening. Some are not. Tom gave this voyage a yeoman's try. The end product, however, had not been enlightenment, but merely dirty sheets. Even though I had played Mentor to Tom's Telemachus, he asked if I would get rid of the evidence.

"Do you want me to burn the sheets?" I asked, half-jokingly.

"No, no, no," he said, as he emerged from the shower. "Could you just take them down to the basement and put them in the washing machine. I'll take care of them in the morning."

It was 4 a.m. Buck naked, I made my way down to Tom's basement. It was also the garage. There was now another car parked next to Tom's MG. It had not been there when we had pulled into the garage around midnight. I found the laundry area and stuffed the shitty sheets in the washer and went back upstairs. We both fell asleep.

We got up around 11 a.m. Tom got the coffee started. He went downstairs to see what he could do with the sheets. A couple of minutes later he came back upstairs. He had the sheets. They were clean, dry, and neatly folded. Even the fitted sheet was folded properly.

"Did you do all this?" Tom asked, as he showed me the stack.

"Are those the sheets from last night? No I just put them in the washing machine. I didn't even start it up."

"Oh my god," Tom said. "I think I know who washed the sheets."

"Who?" I said, as the image of the second car parked in the garage flashed through my mind.

"It must have been my tenant. Nobody else has access to those machines."

"Better call him and thank him," I said.

Tom called his tenant. I could hear only part of the conversation.

"What did he say?" I said, when he hung up.

"He said he was glad to see somebody had a good time last night!"

We went for breakfast at a café in the neighborhood. Large Boston ferns were hanging from the ceiling in the entrance. We were led to an interior courtyard garden, where wrought-iron tables and chairs were set on flagstones. Large jungle plants and vines provided semi-secluded spaces.

When we walked over from Tom's place, the sun was out.

Just when the waiter brought our quiche, the fog drifted in. A fine mist settled down into the courtyard. There was a creaking, mechanical sound. I looked up to see a folding glass ceiling slowly cover the courtyard. The quiche was delish. When the bill was presented, there were two handmade chocolate bonbons on the tray.

"Get those out of my sight," Tom whispered through clenched teeth.

They too were delish.

One morning around ten, the phone rang. It was Tom. Did I have a few hours free? I did.

"I'll send my driver around to pick you up. He has a small something in an envelope for you. It's very mild and doesn't last long. If you want, you can take it when he picks you up. It should be coming on by the time you get there."

"By the time I get where?" I asked.

"St. Mary's Cathedral."

"You mean the Mary Maytag Cathedral," I said. The new Roman Catholic cathedral on Gough Street, constructed in the form of a cross, was more reminiscent of a washing machine agitator than a crucifix.

"That's the one."

"Why are we going to Mary Maytag?"

"We aren't. You are. If you want to."

I wanted to. I wasn't sure why.

"My driver also has a ticket to get you in," Tom said, and hung up.

A ticket? Drugs? St. Mary's Cathedral? What was going on? And what did Tom mean by his driver? I got out the Harris Tweed jacket.

I was waiting on the front steps of my building when a black Ford sedan turned down Clementina Alley. On the door was the official circular seal of the City and County of San Francisco. It pulled over to the side, in front of me. I walked over and smiled at the driver. He wore a dark suit with a white shirt and nondescript tie. His dark hair was cut Marine-jarhead style. He was hot and young.

"Are you Jim?"

I nodded. He leaned over and opened the front passenger door. I got in.

"Here's something from Tom. He says if you take it now it should just be coming on by the time I get you to church."

He handed me a tiny double fold of paper. Very carefully I unfolded it. A miniscule teal-blue translucent square fell into the palm of my hand. I touched the tip of my tongue to it and drew it into my mouth.

"Here's the ticket," the driver said, as he handed me an envelope.

I opened the envelope. It was a ticket alright. It was a ticket to the installation of the new archbishop of the Archdiocese of San Francisco, John R. Quinn.

"What's with this car, and who are you?" I asked as he drove down Clementina and turned right onto 8th Street.

"Well, as you know, Tom, as director, has his own city car. I'm Mark, by the way." He stuck out his hard hand for me to shake as he turned left onto Folsom with his left hand spinning the steering wheel. "I'm in the driver pool. Tom always asks for me. When he can. We ah, understand each other, you might say," he said with a lopsided grin not dissimilar from Tom's. I didn't know, but I understood.

Tom was right. By the time his driver reached the cathedral my eyesight had improved. Things sparkled. It was a beautiful day. I felt very in control. Not jumpy. I followed the crowd toward the main entrance, my ticket in hand. Somewhere, somebody must have taken my ticket, because I realized I no longer had it. I also realized I was inside a giant beehive. The bees were all dressed in medieval robes as the hive ascended into the bright blue sky. Cameramen buzzed about on electric golf carts, their cameras whirring.

It was then I realized that Tom had not really given me a ticket to the installation of the archbishop. He had given me a ticket to the filming of a Fellini movie. Clouds of incense perfumed the set, as men in long robes of white and gold proceeded at a stately pace down aisles toward the center of the universe.

Off to the side, I found a pew and sat down. Suddenly other people on the pew with me arose, and then knelt on a padded prayer bench. We were in the cathedral, after all. I knelt too.

Modern. Medieval. Tradition. Ancient ritual. Golf-cart media. Spaceship cathedral. Ecumenical. Roman Catholic. Orthodox. Greek, Russian, Latin. Episcopal. Lutheran. Sit stand kneel. Stand kneel sit. Kneel sit stand.

More clouds of incense, as the white and gold robes returned the way they had come, back down the aisles. People were standing up now, but they weren't kneeling or sitting back down. They were flowing out into the aisles. They were leaving. It was over. John R. Quinn was officially the Archbishop of San Francisco. My translucent teal-blue transporter was gone. Its time had run out. The beehive spaceship had landed firmly back on Gough Street. Fellini had packed up his cameras and left. I walked outside. It was still a beautiful day, but it no longer sparkled. Yellow cabs were parked along the street. Crowds of people were standing around in front of the cathedral. I got in a cab at the front of the line.

"Ninth and Clementina," I told the cabby. He took off with the obligatory screech of tires. Fog had started to drift in from the Pacific. I looked at my watch. In the four hours since Tom had called, I had passed through millennia.

My mind drifted back to what the city driver had told me, while he drove to the cathedral. So Tom works for the city, I thought, as the cabbie pulled up in front of my place on Clementina. He's a director for the City and County of San Francisco. Director of what, you old rogue, I thought.

The Shapeshifter

I was sitting in the Ambush one afternoon enjoying the crowd. It had been running hot and was still ramping up for Saturday night. My legs spread, my engineer boots propped on the boot rail of the meat rack, I felt hot. I was nursing an Oly, my favorite beer, when I felt my foot being moved. A dark-haired man with a short full beard and mustache was licking my left boot. He was on his knees directly in front of me. He looked up at me with big brown eyes, the whites showing under his dark irises.

"May I clean your boots, sir?"

"Clean 'em up good," I ordered.

Great pickup line! He looked familiar. I thought I had seen him gathering empty beer bottles around the bar and stocking cold ones on ice for the bartenders. Bottle boys, they were called. His dark complexion brought to mind the exotic Mediterranean dives in Marseilles or Tangiers. His accent was French. I thought of a younger, thinner, more handsome Peter Lorre, lurking not around Rick's Place, but the Ambush.

Then he was gone. So much for my boots. I saw him at the bar, talking to Larry Beach, the bartender. Larry looked in my direction. I'd last seen Larry in his Langton Street apartment on the floor with his legs over my shoulders. He had prepared an excellent meal of fresh clams steamed in white wine for the two of us. Larry scowled a dirty look, retrieved something from under the bar, and handed it to my would-be bootblack. The bottle boy came back.

"Bear Grease, sir?" He held out a round tin of non-polish boot dressing for oiled leather. His sinewy hands had already started massaging my foot through the boot. They seemed almost double jointed in their dexterity.

"If you do it right." It'd been awhile since my boots had been properly dressed. The last time I had done it myself.

His hands worked on my boots, massaging my feet through the leather. Finished, he cleaned his hands on a red bandana pulled from his right hip pocket. Those talented hands slowly started up my legs while gently rubbing the top of his head in my crotch. I pulled out a couple of dollars and handed them to my new bootblack.

"Get us a couple of beers," I said.

He was back in a minute with a couple of Olympia longnecks. I nodded to the space on the meat rack next to me. As he hoisted his tight ass up onto the well-worn wood, I noticed his keys hung from the right side of his Levi's. Mine hung from the left. I had a feeling we were headed for a hot night in The Other Room. We finished our beers and went back to my place on Clementina Alley. I was right. Luc instinctively knew what The Other Room was for.

Luc was a moveable feast. Like truffles, a musky scent of mystery hung about him. One day, not too long after we met, he wanted to go to a little hole-in-the-wall Vietnamese restaurant called Cordon Bleu, on California Street. We got in the pickup and headed north.

"I was in Vietnam, once," Luc said, as we watched well-groomed gents window shop on Polk Street. We stopped for a light. A small framed antique oil painting displayed in an art gallery window caught my eye. It depicted a pair of crossed hands bound with a leather thong. Circling the hands was half a halo. The whole looked part of a much larger work that suggested St. Sebastian.

"Hot," I said as I looked at Luc. He too had spotted the painting. He crossed his hands above his head and rolled his eyes heavenward in homage to the beautiful soldier-saint shot full of arrows. The luminescence of the skin on Luc's delicately strong hands did indeed look like they might belong to a third-century martyr. My Nikon waited. The light turned green.

"So how did you end up in Vietnam?" I knew the French had been routed from Dien Bien Phu in 1954. Luc would have been about eight at the time.

"When I was 16 my father was killed in an auto accident. My mother emancipated me. I dropped out of school in Switzerland and decided to travel. I went to Thailand, but ended up on a jungle boat tour that strayed into Vietnam. We were shot at but I learned to love the food."

I did some fast mental calculation. That would have been a couple of years before the Gulf of Tonkin incident in 1964, and the start of the American buildup of the war. Maybe it was possible. I spotted a parking slot on California and maneuvered the truck into the tight space. We got out and headed back to the Cordon Bleu.

It really was a hole-in-the-wall. It was long and narrow, with the door on the far left, and a large window on the right that allowed you to see the entire interior from the sidewalk. Inside was a long counter, with stools mounted on the floor, along one side. It seemed a smaller, scruffier version of Edward Hopper's *Nighthawks.* It was nearly noon. The sun was out. Behind the counter, flames leaped up as chicken fat dripped on the fire below the grill. It was a sideshow for the diners.

We spotted two stools with a man sitting between them. He saw our dilemma, slid his plate and water glass to the left, and graciously gestured toward the two stools now together. We smiled and sat down. A tiny gray-haired woman behind the counter asked us something in a *lingua franca* I did not know. It seemed a mixture of Vietnamese, French, and maybe English. Luc smiled, nodded his head, and replied in kind. He turned to me.

"Do you want the five-spice chicken? It's really good and a good price. It's always their special."

I did.

Luc replied to the woman behind the counter. She grabbed two oval platters from a stack under the counter and scooped what looked like dirty rice onto each. Still holding both platters in one hand, she turned to the grill behind her and, using a pair of tongs, lifted two grilled half chickens off the back of the grill and placed one on top of each of the rice platters. The chickens were small, a bantam breed, but the breasts were large. A dozen or so grilled chicken halves remained on the back of the grill. On the front of the grill, soft white chicken skin puckered as it stretched over the cooking birds. It slowly began to blister and shrink and then hissed when the chicken halves were turned over by a tiny aged man.

The woman turned back to the counter, set the platters in front of us, and, as if by magic, produced a small wicker basket with sourdough baguettes which she set in front of us. This all in less than a minute. She asked Luc something.

"*The*," he replied and then turned to me. "Do you want tea?"

"Yes."

The woman understood my *yes* and set a small steaming vitreous-china pot and two small handless cups in front of us. The smell of oolong tea mingled with the rich five-spice aroma that infused the tiny space.

The chicken was delish. The sweet star-anise reigned. Cinnamon, cloves, and lemony ginger supported the licoriceness of the anise in an exotic fusion. The place, the food, and our hostess, conversing in pidgin French and chattering in Vietnamese, all combined to take us on a trip, while we never left the narrow confines of the hole-in-the-wall.

I was whisked off to some pre-war Saigon side street, seduced, and died a little gourmand death in a city once known as Paris of the East. If fusion be the food of love, eat on. A denouement of beer-battered fried bananas sprinkled with sugar rounded off our repast. The sun was still out as we left the Cordon Bleu.

"Let's take a drive over to Marin County."

"Let's."

I continued west on California to Divisadero, then north to the Marina, where I picked up Highway 101 to cross the Golden Gate Bridge. I glanced down at the old Civil War fort, Fort Point, far below at the south end of the bridge. *Vertigo*, I thought, where Jimmy Stewart once jumped into the bay to rescue Kim Novak from a fake suicide.

Once over the bridge, we headed west, out by the old World War II bunkers on the Marin Headlands. They were the bunkers Jack Fritscher once showed to Robert Mapplethorpe. He shot his leather hood and piss pictures there. I pulled the pickup into an unofficial dust lot, where the adventurous often parked. The fog had come in for the afternoon. Although we were less than a mile from the Golden Gate Bridge, we could only see the very tops of the two towers.

"Want to go down the path there to the bay?" I said. Like the parking lot, it was unofficial, dusty, and eroded. I knew it was easy going down, harder coming up. You had to be careful where you placed each step and look for scrubby wild bushes to hang on to in case the ground gave way.

"Yes," Luc said. "I've never been down there."

Luc knew where to find that little place in Chinatown where you ate in the kitchen, or the little bar that survived both the Gold Rush and the earthquake and still drew San Francisco's lonely men. He knew the best off-Broadway performance art in the City. I knew the wild places, the rambles of bushes in Buena Vista park, the trails at Lands End. Places that had not yet been tamed and controlled by some recreation department or community committee. Places where you could commune with nature *au naturel* while you got it on with your fellow man.

I also knew Ringold Alley, Dore Alley, places for the best impromptu sex after the bars closed at 2:30 a.m. I knew Hallam Alley had a door that led straight into the Barracks baths. Yes, I knew the wild places where you met the wild men of San Francisco in the 1970s, before neighborhood watchers with cell phones reported indecent exposure and lewd acts. You weren't there if it wasn't for lewd and lascivious acts.

We slowly made our way down the eroded path in the fog. No mishaps. No one was there on the narrow dirty beach. Despite the cool air from the fog, we stripped and frolicked in the bay. Muffled foghorns played a coastal score as we made the two-backed beast against a gnarled driftwood tree and died a little death. We heard applause. Ever the actor, Luc stood and bowed. I saluted, with a sheepish grin, to applause and whistled cheers. A fishing boat, returning with the catch of the day, had cut its motor and drifted, silently in the fog, close to shore for the entertainment of the three fishermen onboard.

I'm sure Luc and I provided them all with great fisherman's tales that they traded for free beers and shots wherever they hung out.

In the fall of 1976, President Gerald Ford visited San Francisco. Again. A year earlier, on a trip to California, the unelected-appointed President from Michigan had narrowly missed assassination. Twice. On September 4, 1975, Lynette "Squeaky" Fromme was wrestled to the ground in Sacramento when she tried to take a shot at the President. In San Francisco a couple of weeks later, on September 22nd, when Ford left the St. Francis Hotel by a side door, Sara Jane Moore tried her hand at assassination from four feet away with a .38. Billy Sipple, a gay man still in the closet, deflected Moore's shot and most likely saved the President's life. The press outed Sipple.

California was important to Ford. The state's ex-governor, Ronald Reagan, had tried to steal the GOP nomination from the sitting President. Ford won the Republican Party's top spot. He returned to San Francisco for a GOP fundraiser. The local politicians held court for the President at a fancy downtown hotel, the Sir Francis Drake. My landlord, Clarence, had two tickets to the affair.

"You're from Michigan, aren't you?" Clarence asked me one day.

"Born and bred."

"Are you a Republican?"

My Michigan family's ancestors had voted Republican since Lincoln, probably since John Fremont, if truth be known. I had broken over a century-long family tradition by voting for Lyndon Baines Johnson in 1964.

"I guess you could say I'm an Independent," I said. I had actually registered in San Francisco's City Hall as a Democrat, so I could vote in the primary.

"What do you think of Ford?"

I wasn't sure I liked where this might be headed. There were those who hated Ford for pardoning Nixon. Some thought if you were from Michigan, like Ford, it was somehow all your fault that Nixon hadn't ended up in prison. Clarence must have seen my dilemma.

"The reason I asked," he said, "is that I have two tickets for a Ford fundraiser at the Drake. The President's going to be there.

Now, I wouldn't give that son of a bitch two bits," Clarence continued, "but I hate to throw away the tickets. You can have them if you want. I'm sure there'll be a big buffet and probably an open bar."

"Sure. It might be interesting."

Clarence handed me a small envelope much like a wedding invitation. I pulled the card out of the envelope and ran my finger over the script. It was engraved.

"I don't have to give them any money, do I?"

"They'll give their pitch. Just say no."

"Thanks."

Luc was delighted when I asked him if he would like to meet President Ford. As an actor he had never played a role where he met an American president.

"Do I bow or anything, like meeting the Queen?"

"Only if you want to. You can curtsy if you like."

Luc did a fake curtsy with his best Peter Lorre smile. We both burst out laughing. We decided we should get dressed up a little, even though the occasion was not formal. My old reliable tweed jacket would stand in again. Instead of the Levi's, however, I found a pair of gray flannels that would lend me a certain young professorial air, as if I were on the faculty at Berkeley, or at least San Francisco State.

Luc arrived. He was dashing in an Edwardian Norfolk suit from a smart boutique on the Right Bank in Paris. At the last minute I grabbed my Nikon. We took a cab to the Drake Hotel. We were fashionably late.

There were no lines out the door of the hotel. Inside, when we inquired, we were directed to a side door off the main lobby. Security was everywhere. We were told to wait in a little hallway while our invitation was checked.

"Where did you get this invitation?"

"A friend gave it to me. Is there a problem?"

"Just a moment, please," said a man in a black suit with a suspicious bulge under his jacket. He started to leave the room when an idea struck me.

"I'm from Grand Rapids, Michigan," I raised my voice a little, "and he's on a mission from France." I nodded towards Luc.

Grand Rapids was Gerald Ford's home town. In a few minutes Black-suit returned.

"What's that?" Black-suit asked, pointing to my camera.

"A Nikon," I said, "I'm a photographer from Grand Rapids, and I want to get some pictures of our hometown hero."

Black-suit nodded and took the invitation. We went on into the ballroom. As soon as we were through the door, I realized what part of the problem had been. We did not look like Republicans. Most of the men and the few women in the room had the look of confidence, of privilege, and of the grooming and tailoring that wealth and power convey on people. They did not look at all like the rural Republicans I had grown up among.

The gathering was not nearly as large as I had expected. We helped ourselves to the buffet laden with jumbo shrimp, imported cheeses and what looked like South American grapes and other sundry finger foods. No Cesar Chavez fruit here. Evidently Alice Waters' "local and seasonal" mantra held no sway here either. There was neither California nor imported wine on the table. There was an open bar with mixed drinks and a bartender who I'm sure expected to be well tipped. He exuded that smart, snappy courtier edge-of-gay that causes Republicans to tip well and gays to snicker.

We made our way across the room looking for the President. He was not here. At last, a rising in the volume of the crowd noise gave a clue he had arrived. People started moving toward one end of the room where Ford had evidently entered. We followed them, leaving our plates on some empty chairs. There he was, bigger than life, the President of the United States, POTUS.

Dodging Republicans and black suits I was able to get off a few pictures of the President. I wasn't really satisfied with any of the shots I got, due to the crowd and the black suits that kept within a close circle of POTUS. Black suits kept watching me, as if they thought my Nikon might be Sara Jane Moore's snub-nosed .38.

I ran out of film. I looked around for Luc. Where was he? Then I turned back to the President and saw Luc shaking hands with him. He let go of Ford's famous big football paw and executed a smart stage bow, exactly like the one he had given the voyeuristic fishermen who had caught us *in flagrante delicto* on the beach in the fog a week before. Luc had played his role of meeting the President of the United States to perfection and then taken his bow. He didn't curtsy, any way. He spotted me and came over.

"Here," I said. "take the camera. I haven't shaken hands with him yet." I made my way through the crowd and did just that. Somehow it seemed anticlimactic. The true theater had been gaining entrance and Luc's perfect stage bow in front of the President. I had pictures of POTUS. And we both had shaken the hand of the most powerful man on Earth.

We left the Drake Hotel and took a cab to the Ambush. Luc, the Parisian dandy, soon left with a Francophile. They were off to do what? Something French? Perhaps sip Armagnac, smoke hashish, and read Rimbaud while lounging naked on an Aubusson carpet? I stayed, feeling overdressed at the Ambush.

"Hey dad!"

I looked up. Looking down was a youth, no more than 21 or 22. He had let his dark hair and beard grow, untrimmed. He looked a hippie leftover from The Haight a decade ago.

"Want to buy a starving grad student a beer?"

"Get us two," I said. I handed him two singles. "Tip the bartender," I said. "He's a friend of mine."

He returned with a couple of beers.

"So what are you doing your grad work in?" I said as he squeezed his young butt onto the meat rack next to me.

"Poli sci, at San Francisco State."

"Poli sci. You might be interested in this hand," I said.

"You're right there, dad." He grabbed my right hand. He didn't shake it but rather wrapped his fingers around it as if measuring its girth. I made a fist with my fingers pointing out. He started stroking it.

"Do you know what this hand did just an hour ago?" I said.

"Tell me about it," he said. I could see by the growing bulge in his Levi's he was interested.

"This hand shook the hand of POTUS," I said.

"Who's POTUS?"

"President of the United States," I said.

"Not Gerry Ford! Not the man who can't chew gum and

walk at the same time? The most powerful man on Earth? Not the POTUS who fathered those hot sons who go camping nude?"

"The very same." President Ford had been caught on camera stumbling down the steps from Air Force One. Despite the fact he had been captain of the University of Michigan football team in his youth, and still kept his athlete's body buff, he had earned the reputation of clumsy. The press had also caught the First Sons on a camping trip, where one appeared to be naked, in the bushes.

"Have you washed your hands since you shook his?"

"No." I realized where this was going. The young hippie continued to caress my right hand with his while he reached over for my left hand and brought it down to his now very evident hard-on.

"We'll go to my place," I said. "It's only a couple of blocks away."

It didn't take us long to get to The Other Room. I told him to strip. I stepped out of the room and removed the Harris Tweed jacket. I replaced it with a dark blue pinstripe vest. I kept on the gray flannels, oxford shirt and black knit tie. As I came back into the room I saw my young hippie naked, on the floor. I lifted his head up by his long hair.

He watched as I slowly rolled up my right sleeve to my bicep. "There are those," I said, "who believe that great power can be transferred from male to male just by body contact." I paused while I formed an elongated fist with my right hand and slowly stroked it with my left. "You know when I shook hands with POTUS I absorbed power from him. Right through this hand," I said, as I held up my right fist.

"Would you like some of his power too?" I said, as I arched my eyebrows and stared into his dark eyes. Young Hippie nodded his head affirmatively. It sent ripples cascading down his long dark hair. I gently pushed him back onto the mattress on the floor and knelt between his legs. He placed them on my shoulders. I spit in my right hand and gently began to massage his hairless pink male-bud. We started our own inaugural ball and the transfer of power from man to man.

By beating a drum roll with my left fist on my right arm, the vibrations carried the power of POTUS from one man into the very core of another. Sometimes men are totally unaware of the power they pass on through just two degrees of separation. Perhaps that's why ancient chiefs sometimes buried their excrement in secret holy places to prevent their enemies from stealing their power.

Christmas was coming. It was my second Christmas in San Francisco. The previous Christmas, from a house in Marin County that overlooked the Pacific, I had watched whales migrate south. A black leather cat-o'-nine-tails played over my bare butt and back. After moving to San Francisco, I'd learned of endorphins and the pleasures of pain. It wasn't unlike the runner's high I had experienced while jogging. Receiving pain, I learned how to give it. Because it was Christmas I got to keep the cat-o'-nine-tails. I also got to keep the grand gift of knowledge it brought.

This year, Christmas would be more traditional. I already had my wrapping paper and name tags. The paper I found in the printer's dumpster on Clementina Alley. It was a roll of rejects: large sheets of sepia-tone photos of run-down motels, mom-and-pop diners and other roadside attractions in Arizona along a stretch of what was once the Father Road, Route 66. Half were printed upside down to the others, so when folded in a folio, they all turned out right. They made great giftwrapping paper.

The nametags came from the 1941 Alameda County Fair. I bought a box of blue ribbons for a buck at the flea market. Everyone's a winner this year, I thought. It was 1976.

A friend of mine from Michigan had moved to San Francisco. Joelle, like me, had been in a straight, child-free marriage. She divorced and moved to San Francisco, to see what else life had to offer.

She was single. It was her first Christmas in the City. While I did not plan to introduce her to the pleasures of pain, or even watch migrating whales with her, we did want to do something special; something neither of us had done before. Joelle, Luc and I would go to Grace Cathedral for Midnight Mass on Christmas Eve.

Grace Episcopal Cathedral sits atop Nob Hill in its neo-*Notre*

Dame de Paris splendor. Although it took over half of the 20th century to build, it exudes the mystique of what Luc called the "old stones" of Europe. The services there are noted for their inclusion of universal extra-Christian beliefs.

Rampant rumor had it, a secret Christian cannibal cult inhabited the nether regions, as well as the soaring vaulted rafters of Grace Cathedral, in a sort of *Hunchback-of-Notre-Dame* meets *Phantom-of-the-Opera* fantasy. The Cathedral boasted, in the centuries-old Anglican tradition, one of the finest men's and boys' choirs this side of the Atlantic.

In short, it was perfect for a special Christmas Eve in San Francisco. Midnight Mass at Grace Cathedral would be the best show in town.

Christmas Eve Mass started at 11 p.m. The three of us took a cab from Clementina Alley. Luc and I wore the outfits we had worn to President Ford's fundraiser: Parisian dandy and elbow-patch professor. Joelle wore a slightly dyke-y navy linen suit with white jabot and sensible librarian shoes. Her short blond hair and whisper of makeup said she'd been around and could go down. Elegantly.

We arrived at the cathedral on California Street a little after 10 o'clock. The main entrance was closed. Off to the side, a not-so-long-line was filing through a small door. We followed the line and soon were inside. The nave was packed. We were able to squeeze in on the end of a pew by a side aisle. As our eyes adjusted to the dim interior that seemed to be lit solely by candlelight, we started focusing on who was there.

People-watching is a great pastime anywhere, but in San Francisco it is a fine art. There were scores of handsome young men dressed in their Sunday best. Most came in pairs, accompanied by a well-groomed matronly woman. Mothers, I thought. Mothers here to visit their gay sons for Christmas. Were they the ghosts of musical comedies past?

Joelle leaned over and whispered in my ear. "I hope nobody thinks I'm your mother!"

Luc, sitting on her other side said, in a very French-accented stage whisper, "Mama, are you enjoying San Francisco?"

I stifled a laugh as a matronly woman in front of us turned

and glared.

The organ music shifted as regal strains of "O Come All Ye Faithful" sounded throughout the cavernous sanctuary. Male voices in holy harmony filled the cathedral with Latin verse, as the Grace Cathedral Choir of Men and Boys slowly made its way past us on the side aisle, before they turned into the central aisle to approach the altar and the choir stalls beyond. As they passed, I inhaled deeply. The slight smell of seminal musk filled my nostrils. Their voices rang out in harmony.

Adeste fideles
laeti triumphantes;
Venite, venite in Bethlehem.

In its ecumenical way, the Episcopalian cathedral must have considered Latin still acceptable for Christmas mass. I joined them under my breath for the chorus.

Venite adoremus,
Venite adoremus,
Venite adoremus,
Dominum.

That was about all I could remember from high school Latin. Incense (once thought to purify the air and drive away the evil spirits from the unwashed medieval masses who packed the ancient basilicas on high holy days) followed the clean-sweat smell of the all-male choir.

It mingled with the smoke and beeswax smell of holy tapers, whose light glinted off the rich gold and silver embroidered stoles and white lace surplices, as all proceeded through the ancient rituals proclaiming the glories of an immaculate birth. It was indeed the best show in town.

When it ended, we took a cab back to Clementina Alley. We had the driver let us out at the corner. Luc headed down Clementina to the flat. I needed cigarettes from the Lebanese mom-and-pop store on the corner. Joelle came with me to the store. Mom and pop had two incredibly handsome eastern Mediterranean sons.

Even though it was well past midnight on Christmas Eve, the store was still open. It would probably stay open until 2 a.m. when liquor sales were cut off by law.

The younger son was behind the counter, in front of the cigarettes and liquor. I had flirted with him several times and when he was alone he would flirt back.

"Merry Christmas, Amiel," I said. They were Lebanese Christians. "Two packs of Marlboros, please." I smiled at him and he smiled back fetchingly.

"Jim," Joelle said, "Let's get a bottle of Courvoisier. It's Christmas Eve."

"And a pint of Courvoisier cognac," I added, pointing to it on the shelf behind the counter.

Amiel looked at Joelle, then back at me, then smiled at Joelle.

"Are you sure a pint will be enough?" he said, with a devilish smirk.

"It's Christmas," I said. "Give me a full bottle. There are three of us."

"Three!" Amiel laughed. "You naughty man!" He reached behind him for a full bottle of Courvoisier. "Merry Christmas."

Joelle burst out laughing as we left the store and headed for Clementina Alley.

Luc was an actor. He had studied acting at a private school in Switzerland. He played many roles in his travels, including that of a young lover for a Bedouin chieftain, during a caravan trip across North Africa.

When he settled in London for awhile, when it was the swinging capital of the western world, he formally studied acting again. After he moved to San Francisco he had trouble finding parts. He was once asked if he would like to join Our Sisters of Perpetual Indulgence, a group of "drag nuns," just to keep his hand in some sort of acting. He declined.

Luc did keep abreast of off-Broadway and experimental theater productions in the Bay Area. He auditioned for anything he thought he had a chance at. As a result, we ended up attending a lot of small theater productions.

Long before Derek Jarman's film, we saw Marlowe's *Edward II* in what seemed a leatherman's dungeon. There were benches for about 30 people. We all sat packed and sweaty with anticipation as the play unfolded from a stage set of the ass-end of a semi-trailer parked on a foggy loading dock. Welded chain curtains, like those found in such rigs, divided the space for various scenes.

After this Teamsters' production, we returned to the flat on Clementina to reenact the roles of Edward and Piers Gaveston. Off-off-Broadway stage and The Other Room melded into our own personal performance space.

Another play, *Wolf Lodge*, I believe, perhaps in honor of Jack London, took place in an isolated B&B lodge under the redwoods of Sonoma County. Once the guests all retired and the embers burned low, the "wolves" came out to howl, dance, and play with pulley, hoist, and leather sling. Luc and I also followed this production with an encore in The Other Room on Clementina Alley.

One day, when I was in the darkroom, printing sets of photos of my Keyhole Studio models to send to sexually starving lonely men in the hinterlands, I heard Luc come up the stairs and into the flat.

"I got the part," he hollered through the door.

"Which one?"

"Count Orlov!"

"I'll be right out." I finished and came out of the bathroom I had set up as a darkroom.

"There's only one thing," Luc added as we headed for the kitchen in the back of the flat for coffee and cigarettes. "They want me to shave my head."

"Great," I said. "You'll look hot with a shaved head!"

"I don't know..."

"I'll tell you something about a shaved head, Luc. When I had my head shaved I instantly became so-hot-got-to-have-you for a whole gang of guys that hadn't even looked at me before."

"Well..."

"Of course there were those who acted like they didn't know me after my head was shaved."

"Maybe they didn't. That's what I'm afraid of."

"Luc, I've never known you to be afraid of anything in your life. You're going to be as hot as a billiard ball up Sal Mineo's ass."

"Will you shave it for me?"

"Damn right I'll shave you. We're going to do it in the

playroom as a three-way. I'm going to take pictures. Who's the hottest man you can think of to be on third?"

"Malcolm," Luc said, without a moment's hesitation.

"Hot damn! Malcolm is perfect."

I had done some carpentry and plumbing work for Malcolm at his house in Bernal Heights. He was about 6-3 and had a natural-muscle body. I saw a picture of him once when he had been on the university rowing team at Stanford. It was one of those sports group pictures. All the crew members were in singlets or shirtless, with their arms around each other, thrusting their baskets in tight shorts toward the camera lens. Malcolm was a standout to say the least. With his dark complexion and short-clipped curly hair, he might have been mistaken for Harry Belafonte's younger brother. Hot.

When I worked for Malcolm, we had always hinted at a scenario. He would come home from the office early one day. I, the carpenter, would be caught in a compromising position. It had never happened. Shaving Luc's head while in a three-way with Malcolm in The Other Room was my idea of perfect personal performance theater, where the performers and audience were one.

"I'll call Malcolm."

It was a perfect performance. To peel Luc's scalp, I used a pair of barber scissors and a World War I army issue safety razor in a khaki kit I found at the Alameda flea market.

The coup de grâce was performed by my great-grandfather's Victorian straight razor. It was sharpened with a leather strop that performed many additional duties that night, and provided staccato sound effects that punctuated the rhythm of the fuck-tape. I was right. Luc looked hot with a shaved head. Not a nick on it. The best photo of the night was one I shot of Luc, very tentatively touching his shaved head for the first time, as if discovering a new self he had never known before.

When John Eli and I had our heads shaved at the Slot bathhouse in 1976, we left the door open. All could see and be turned on by what they saw. Jack Fritscher directed, for those who wanted to participate. In the parlance of the day it was "A Happening." I took photos of the Slot shaving that were published in *Drummer* magazine, Issue 16, 1977.

Luc's head shaving, in the privacy of The Other Room on Clementina, a year later, was a personal piece to embrace the "joy of now." When I shaved David Wyckoff's head on top of a white metal hospital bed, with piss collected in an army canteen in the Leatherneck Bar, in 1978, while Greg Coats shot Caravaggio tableaus in color, it was "performance art."

By 1981, when the Drummer bar, Gold Coast West, opened a barber shop for body and head shaves, done to the soundtrack of *Sweeney Todd: The Demon Barber of Fleet Street*, and videocast live to screens in the main bar room, such shavings had crossed over into the mainstream of leather life South of Market, as it was nudged into what would become SoMa. It all was captured on film.

Luc played his role of Count Orlov well. With his shaved head, he looked and acted the Russian count, ousted by the Bolsheviks, and exiled to British bourgeois drawing rooms between the wars.

It was a vapid play, produced on a small rehearsal stage at the Palace of Fine Arts between the Marina and the Presidio. It got Luc back on stage. I took pictures. Luc kept looking for roles that fit his dark fetching looks and universal European accent. He never found them. We did discover a lot of interesting theater along the way, however.

Fort Mason, built during the Civil War near the Marina, was the debarkation point for thousand of servicemen bound for the Pacific Theater during the Second World War. By the 1970s it had been taken over by the National Park Service, as part of the Golden Gate National Recreation Area. It was converted into an arts center with a view of Alcatraz and the Golden Gate Bridge.

The Magic Theatre of Berkeley was one of the first nonprofit groups to move into Fort Mason. Its production of Sam Shepard's *Inacoma* was a must-see for Luc. *Inacoma* was based loosely on the real-life case of Karen Ann Quinlan, a brain-dead woman whose parents went to court to have her life support system turned off. Shepard's play evolved as a joint production of actors and jazz musicians. The musicians would stand behind the actors who could not act until the musicians would play, and conversely, at times the musicians could not play until the actors would act. Theatergoers left humming the closing song, "Breathing Forever." I left the theater convinced Shepard's work was similar to the personal performance pieces I had begot in The Other Room on Clementina Alley.

I had asked Max Morales to make a tape for me, from his vast and varied music collection. I called it "fuck-tape." I wanted it to build from foreplay to climax within an hour, and then automatically replay at the same building pace. This way I could keep track of the time for those guests in The Other Room who tipped by the hour.

I did not want the popular disco tunes of the day. The more esoteric and exotic and erotic the music, the better. Max, who had been making tapes for clubs and happenings for some time, knew exactly what I wanted. His tapes were superb. I could improvise the trip in The Other Room according to the music and the people involved.

It was what Sam Shepard was doing with *Inacoma.* Max, who had gone to the Fort Mason production with us, agreed with my comparison. The big difference being our productions were staged privately, South of Market, for a more select group.

Shortly before Luc moved to New York, we decided one night to visit a little gay cabaret on Polk near Bush Street. It was a hole in the wall, with a dozen tiny tables at the most. The tables were just big enough to hold drinks for four people. The show had received good reviews in the gay rags. The performers had live music. They were live drag. No lip-synch. And, as in *Cabaret,* "every one of them a virgin!"

Even though there was no cover, no minimum, the place was nearly empty when we arrived in our full black leathers just before 11 p.m. We got a table next to the slightly raised stage. We ordered our drinks. We were both good at nursing a drink.

The first act was almost finished when there seemed to be a flurry of activity behind us by the door. Suddenly the owner was at our table.

"Gentlemen," he said, "a special guest and his party have just arrived." I turned to look near the door, but it was too dark. Four figures loomed just outside the aureole of light from the stage.

"If you gentlemen would be willing to move to the table right over there," he nodded to another small table, further back from the stage but still in a good location, "your drinks will be on the house for the night."

Drinks on the house for the night? I looked at Luc. He had already stood up and was following the waiter carrying our drinks to the other table. Four men in suits were seated at the tiny table we had just left. My eyes adjusted to the darkness away from the stage while its light illuminated the faces of the "special guests."

I nudged Luc. "See anybody who looks familiar?" I said.

Luc turned around . "Is that the mayor?" he said.

"In the flesh." We had just given up our table in a hole-in-the-wall gay night club to Mayor George Moscone and three of his pals/bodyguards.

It was an open secret that the mayor and his pals often prowled the seedy side of the City, looking for secrets of the senses. How could anyone govern a city so full of secrets?

There was no nursing of drinks that night.

When we got back to Clementina Alley, Luc had a gift waiting for me. I carefully removed the plain brown wrapper. There was the antique painting of the bound hands and halo of St. Sebastian we'd seen in the gallery on Polk Street that day we went to the Cordon Bleu for Vietnamese five-spice chicken.

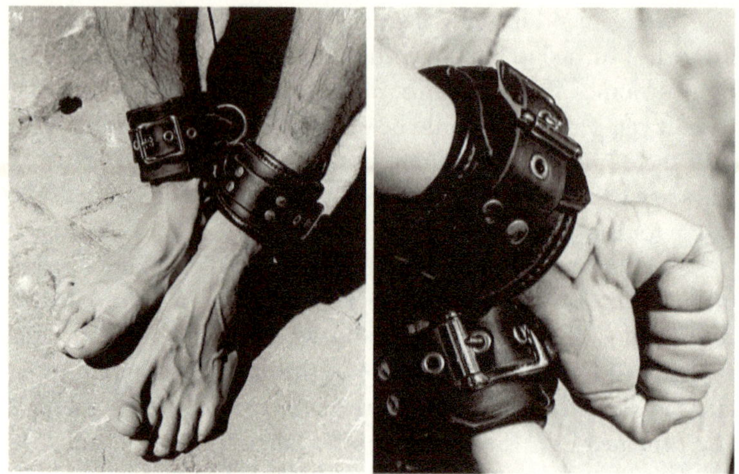

Bound Feet and Bound Hands

1978: model Luc Alexandre, photos by Jim Stewart
shot at the Geysers, Sonoma County, California

Luc at the Pacific Ocean

1978: model Luc Alexandre, photo by Jim Stewart
shot near Jenner by the sea at the Russian River

Five Spice Chicken

Vietnamese hole-in-the-wall
acclaimed as *Cordon Bleu*
off Polk Street on California
in the City of St. Francis

A musky scent of mystery
perfumes the well-worn counter
with pedestals as stools
a smaller, seedier *Nighthawks* café

Flames leap up as fat
spits and drips on fire
below an ancient grill
sideshow for a late lunch

In a *lingua franca*
spoken in borderlands
both East and West
a wizened woman asks
five-spice chicken

They nod yes as she scoops clumps
of rice onto chipped platters
and with a pair of tongs
takes from the grill two tiny chickens
that waft rich decadent aromas

Sweet star-anis reigns
while cinnamon and cloves
with licorice undertones
support freshly grated ginger
in an exotic fusion
more powerful than poppies

Vet and grown boat boy are whisked off
to some imaginary wartime Saigon side street
seduced and die a gourmand's death
in a city once known as Paris of the East

Not sated yet they leave
and retire to a quickly rented room
in the blighted gritty Tenderloin
for a long and languid
lazy *digestif*

Jim Stewart – Photos

1979: announcement for photo exhibit at the Ambush bar, 1351 Harrison St., photo by Jim Stewart of Douglas Tilden sculpture Baseball Player (1889) in Golden Gate Park

Leatherneck Bartender Ron

1977: photo by Jim Stewart,
at the corner of 11th Street and Folsom

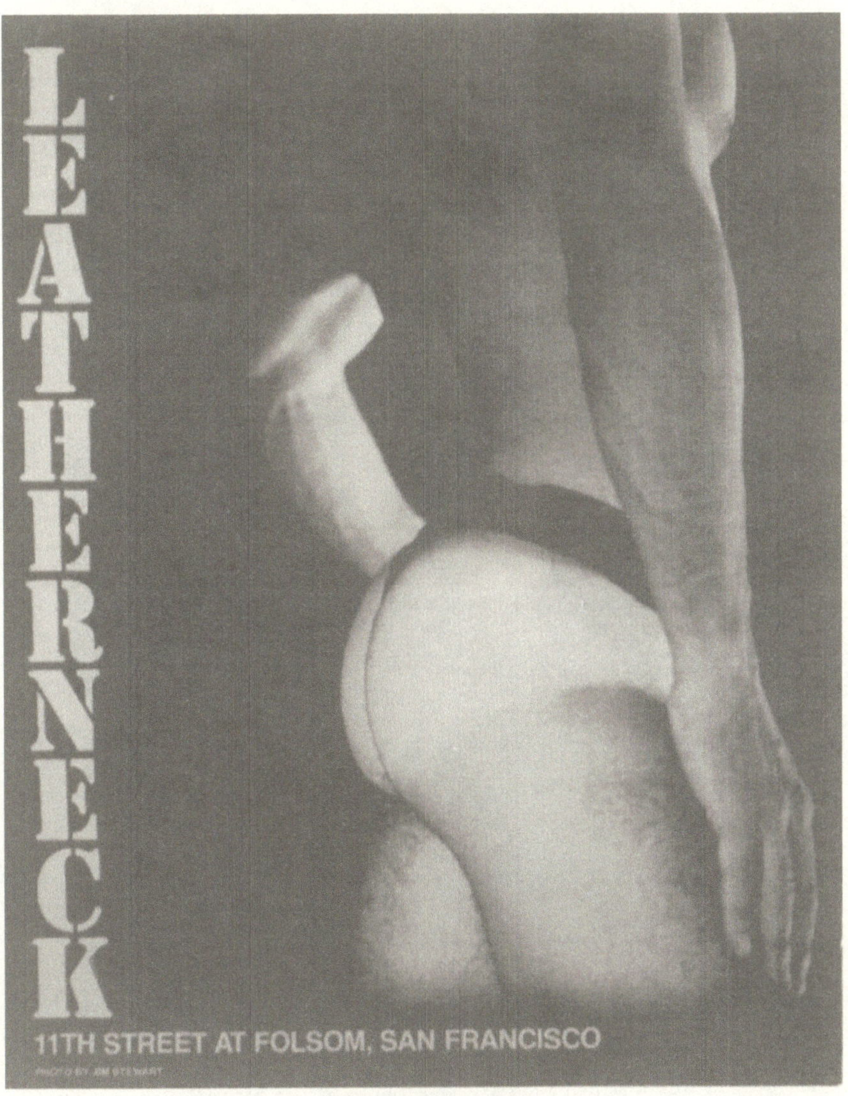

Leatherneck Poster

1977: model Max Morales, photo by Jim Stewart
Published in *Drummer*, Issue 21, p. 78

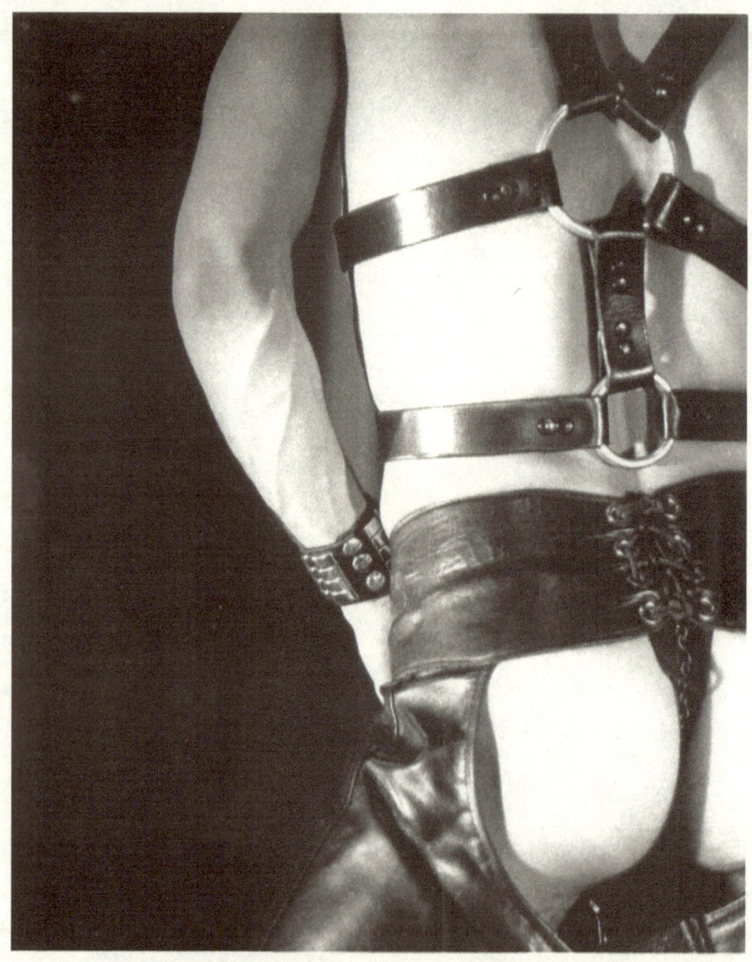

Spring — from the series **Four Seasons of Ass**
1977: model Max Morales, photo by Jim Stewart

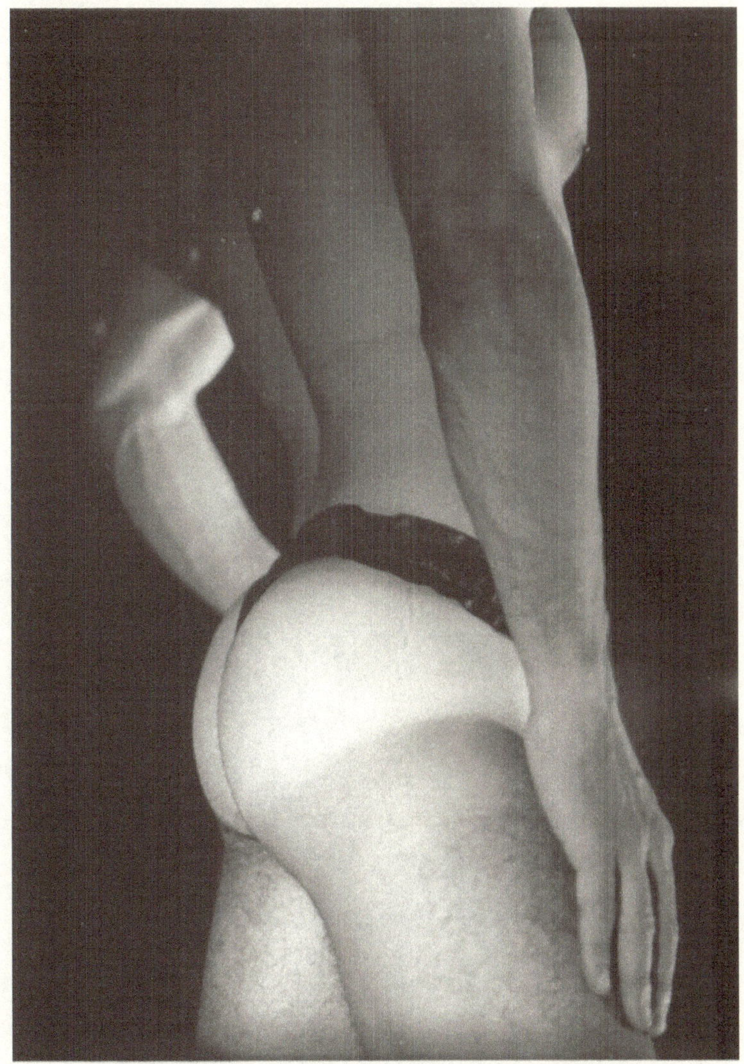

Summer — from the series **Four Seasons of Ass**

1977: model Max Morales, photo by Jim Stewart

Fall — from the series **Four Seasons of Ass**
1977: model Max Morales, photo by Jim Stewart

Winter — from the series **Four Seasons of Ass**

1977: model Max Morales, photo by Jim Stewart

Max for Mr. CMC — 1978

1978: model Max Morales, photo by Jim Stewart
Leatherneck Bar, 11th Street at Folsom
poster for the CMC Carnival

Voodoo

When Allan Lowery opened the Leatherneck bar at 11th and Folsom he hired Rocky as a barback. Barbacks are like sous chefs. They make the bartenders shine. Barbacks make sure the beer coolers behind the bar are well stocked, they give the bartenders breaks during slow times, and pretty much anything else they might want. Bartenders were stars who couldn't shine without good barbacks. Barbacks were like sous chefs.

Before Allan opened the Leatherneck, I constructed meat racks, restraint structures, a cross, and other accoutrements that turned the space into a leather bar. I was the Leatherneck's carpenter. As the crowds grew, and the lines waiting to get in got longer, a second serving bar was needed. Allan asked me to build it in the back room.

It was small. There was just enough space for a couple of washtubs full of ice to chill the longneck beer bottles, a service counter, and a cash drawer. It would take pressure off star bartenders at the main bar and keep the men coming back. If customers wait too long for a beer, they leave. I designed and assembled a hot little bar. It was similar to the four-poster beds for bondage at The Slot. It was done in a day. There was one problem. Allan had no bartender lined up to man it.

"Want to tend bar in the back room tonight?" Allan said upstairs in his office when I told him the project was done.

"Sure," I said. I'd never tended bar in my life. It was just a beer/wine bar, I thought. How hard could it be?

"I'll give you Rocky as your barback," Allan said.

If there had been any doubts in my mind about being a bartender, they vanished at the thought of Rocky being my barback.

Rocky was a poster boy for a Folsom Street bar. He'd celebrated his 21st birthday but not his 30th. He sported close-cropped dark wavy hair and a perpetual five o'clock shadow. He worked without a shirt. Standing next to him, you could feel the heat radiating from his sculptured body. He was a prince from *West Side Story.*

Most men like Rocky come with attitude. He didn't. He was a photographer's dream. I know. I snapped a dozen shots or more of Rocky in nothing but a studded black leather dog collar.

Jack Fritscher and I joined forces for a spread on the Leatherneck in *Drummer* magazine, Number 18, 1977. Jack wrote of the hardass cruising at the Leatherneck. It was San Francisco's ultimate bar of the 1970s, he wrote. After reading that the "Leatherneck ain't exactly fantasy," and that the "Leatherneck trip is real," you knew you better get your ass over there or you'd miss the whole last quarter of the 20th century.

Just in case anyone still had doubts, I photographed the entire staff partying in the Leatherneck after hours. Although the bartenders, Chris and Ron, were hot—especially the shot I got of them pinching each other's nipples—Rocky was the real star of that photo spread. In just three photos, Rocky stole the show. I shot him from the rear, polishing boots. He didn't grovel. He was standing up, to show the perfect muscle-V where his back meets his bare butt. I shot him hanging from the cross I'd built at the end of the bar. Later, for my Double Exposure photo show, I flipped the negative of Rocky on the cross and printed two Rocky malefactors facing each other across a leather-bound crucifix. A triptych for the 1970s. The photo that brought the Rocky fans to the Leatherneck, however, was the one I shot of him buck naked behind the bar. His uncut cock was laid out along the bar next to his thumb. Guys brought steel carpenter tapes to the bar just so they could measure Rocky's thumb and calculate the length of his tool.

A client of mine, Father Jack from San Jose, became enamored with Rocky when he saw him in the *Drummer* spread. I took Father Jack to the Leatherneck one night. I covered for Rocky at the front bar while the priest tongue-polished the malefactor's boots in the back toilet. Rocky received an extra generous tip for allowing the good father to express his admiration.

I arrived at the Leatherneck fifteen minutes early my first

night of bartending. I was to open the back bar at 11 p.m. When I picked up my cash drawer in Allan's office, he had something special for me.

"Want a little toot before you go on?" he said.

"Sure, why not." I'd snorted coke once before, with Bill Essex, when we'd first met. It didn't make me feel hazy the way a joint did. I just felt great, only better. Allan laid out four lines on a mirror tile on his desk top. Two for each of us. He handed me a rolled-up hundred-dollar bill. Since it was his treat, I got to pick which two lines I wanted. I chose the two shorter ones. I was new at this.

"You'll need this if we're as busy as I think we'll be in that back room."

Allan was right. We were busy as hell in the back room. If it hadn't been for that toot, and Rocky keeping me stocked with beer and ice, I never would have made it through to closing time at 2:30 a.m. My tips came out to twice as much as I got paid for the shift. I shared them with Rocky, as was the custom. There were bonuses better then tips, however. I met a man with a shaved head called Tuffy Turtletail. He was a super-realist artist who drew jockstraps hanging on clotheslines. I met a poet from England who taught at Berkeley. Thom Gunn wrote about sex at the Geysers in Sonoma County. I wanted to go.

Best of all, I had Rocky waiting on me all night. He worked stripped to the waist. Sweat poured down his torso as he made his way through the packed mass of male flesh, keeping my bar stocked. I discovered the high one gets being a bartender in a hot bar. I liked it. It was better than a runner's high.

San Francisco in the 1970s was home to hordes of expats from around the world. Many hung out South of Market. These expatriates were quite different from immigrant families from Mexico and the Philippines or the Vietnamese boat people.

Expats usually arrived in San Francisco unburdened with family. Often they brought independent incomes. Most were single. A lot were gay. Some were leathermen. They found San Francisco a better place to live than where they came from.

Tony Baker was such an expat. Luc, himself an expat from Belgium-Switzerland-France-the-World, introduced me to Tony. He spoke with a British accent.

"Are you from England?" I said.

"No," he said, with a charming smile, as if playing a pleasant joke on me.

"Australia," I said in triumph. "I bet you're from Australia." There were lots of gay Australians who made their way to the City for a vacation and stayed.

"No," Tony said again, as he gave Luc a sly wink.

"You have some sort of accent," I said, becoming frustrated. "What do you speak?"

"I speak Empire," Tony said, then laughed.

"You speak Empire?"

"I grew up in Kenya. We left when it was given home rule."

Tony was not the only one who spoke Empire. Bill Essex introduced me to a friend of his, John. He and his sister, Anne, had left Rhodesia after Ian Smith had declared its independence in defiance of Britain. The family left Rhodesia, but had to leave part of their fortune behind. They had already transferred considerable sums into British banks before their move. Anne settled in London, when it was the place to be in the 1960s. John came to San Francisco.

Once a year the brother and sister would meet in what was still Rhodesia and spend as much money as they could in a month, entertaining friends still there. John maintained a suite at his sister's place in London. At John's place on Church Street there was Anne's Room.

One day I got a postcard from John. It was postmarked San Francisco. It looked like it had been torn from the Personals section of the want ads. Sandwiched between more salacious ads, circled by a red pencil, was the announcement: "GWM commands you to celebrate his big four oh." A date and address on Church Street were given. "Activities begin @ 11 p.m. Be there. That's an order."

An offer I couldn't refuse.

One of the bartenders at the Leatherneck was caught with his hand in the till. It was very clever how he pulled it off. Since he was a star, no one thought to watch him. He brought in lots of business. That was the tip-off. He had a lot more customers than were indicated by his register tapes. There was no smoking gun.

Allan decided to hire a private investigator. Right out of Dashiell Hammett. San Francisco, fog, the seedy side of the City. This private Dick didn't wear a threadbare trench coat and weather-worn fedora. He wore black leather chaps and a motorcycle jacket. Those who saw him lusted in their loins for this bad boy. He sat at the bar. Always paid for his own drinks. At closing time he left alone. After a week he reported to Allan what he had discovered.

The beautiful blond bartender from Appalachia had used the principle of the abacus to shortchange the till. When two customers would order a drink of the same price, he would ring it up only once. This wasn't hard in a beer/wine bar. Each customer assumed what he saw rung up was for his drink, if he bothered to look at all. Money for both drinks was put in the till. To keep track of how many drinks were not rung up but money put in the register, a crude abacus was used by stacking quarters from his tips. When coins got low in the till, he would "sell" quarters to the till for fives or tens, which would then go into his tip jar. He knew how much extra to take from the till for the drinks not rung up by the position of his silver-quarter abacus. At the end of the shift his register tapes always matched his cash drawer to the penny. The other bartenders' tapes and cash drawers never matched to the penny.

With the blond bombshell gone, Rocky was promoted to full bartender at the front bar. I lost a hot barback but not for long. Juan was my new barback. He was of the Taos Pueblo in New Mexico. Georgia O'Keeffe had once hired him as a houseboy. She liked young men to work naked around her estate. He was studying to be an opera singer.

"Did you ever try peyote?" I said one night, during a slow period at the bar.

"You mean mescaline?" he said.

I nodded. I guessed they were the same.

"I did my vision quest with peyote buttons I had collected in the desert. I went up in the mountains for three days," he said.

"What happened?"

"I discovered my special gift." He looked up at me with a soft innocent smile.

Dare I ask? "What is your special gift, Juan?"

"Singing," he said. Again with that innocent smile. "That's why I'm studying voice."

After the bar closed, the cash register banks counted, the coolers stocked and the floor swept, I asked Juan if he would like to come over to my place. It was nearly 3:30 in the morning.

"I have to go home now. I have voice lessons in the morning. I need sleep."

Any vision quests of my own would have to wait.

Allan was on a much-needed vacation. He had promoted me to bar manager before he left. One evening, while I was in the upstairs office preparing the cash drawers for the bartenders, I heard somebody unlock the front door and enter the bar. I quickly put the cash drawers back in the safe, closed it and spun the dial. I turned out the office light and slipped out the door. There were three rooms on the second floor. The first two were toilets. The one at the end was the office.

I stood in the dark on the narrow balcony that was the passageway for the three rooms. The cavernous room below was lit by just a few dim lights near the sinks under the bar.

Somebody was walking around down below. I saw him go to the meat racks, pull out a beer case and remove a bottle. It was full. It was room temperature. Why would anyone want a warm beer? I watched as he opened the bottle, put his thumb over the top and shook it.

By now my eyes had adjusted to the dark interior of the bar. I could see who it was. It was Rocky.

I watched as he walked to first one corner of the room and then the others. At each corner he shook the beer bottle and then slightly lifted his thumb and allowed some beer to spray out. He was moving his arm in some configuration while he did this. It wasn't until the third time I realized what he was doing. Rocky was spraying the sign of the cross into each corner of the room.

I was intrigued.

I didn't want to disturb him during some personal religious rite he might be performing. On the other hand, I was curious. He headed for the double front doors that were below the balcony. I crept down the narrow curved stairway that wrapped down to the main floor. I heard the hiss of warm beer as it was released against the front doors.

I didn't want to startle Rocky, so I stomped my boots rather loudly on the last three steps as I came down.

"Hello?" I called out as if I wasn't sure who it might be.

"Hi," Rocky said, sounding only a little surprised.

There was a long moment of silence as I looked at his glistening torso in the dim bar light. Some of the beer was running down his naked chest. Had he sprayed himself with a cross as well? I couldn't wait any longer.

"What were you doing," I said, in my best nonjudgmental tone.

"My grandmother told me to do it," he said in a perfectly level tone, as if that explained everything.

"Why?" I said, hoping yet to get an explanation.

"The crowds here haven't been as large as they used to be. I think that new bar, the Black and Blue, over on Howard, is drawing a lot of our customers away."

I nodded agreement.

"My tips are way down."

Again I nodded my understanding.

"I asked my grandmother if she could do anything about it. She told me to spray the cross at the door. It would attract more people. I thought maybe the cross in the corners would help too."

"What is that, Rocky?" I said. "A religious rite?"

His eyes lit up and he smiled showing his perfect white teeth in the dim light.

"Yeah. Santeria."

I felt the same excited uneasiness I had one night years before when I was an undergrad. Then, I'd had two different dates on the same night. One with a good girl, one with a bad girl. Now it was Saturday night again. I was slated to attend a Puerto Rican Santeria ceremony in the Mission at eight and a rich white Rhodesian's 40th birthday party at eleven.

Rocky met me outside the double storefront on Guerrero in the Mission District about a quarter to eight. He was dressed in white, wearing sandals. A small crucifix hung in the open V of his shirt and winked at me in the streetlight. I had on my "dress" black leather pants, a midnight-blue longsleeved police shirt, and a black leather vest. I wore black engineer boots. No crucifix. We went inside.

The wall between the two storefronts had been removed to provide one large room. The walls and ceiling were painted white. The narrow maple flooring had been sanded and refinished. It was patched in the middle where the wall had been removed. Heavy white drapes were pulled across the street windows. Near the back were two doors that must have led to the back rooms and yard.

A wooden table between them held a collection of candles. Candlelight gleamed off small statuettes and a bottle of Bacardi Gold. Beside the rum lay a large cigar. Above the table hung a faintly foreign picture of a saintly woman. Was it the Madonna or perhaps some virginal martyr from the Caribbean? I couldn't tell.

When we entered, Rocky was immediately greeted by several extremely handsome and beautiful young people, of both sexes. All wore white. Everybody seemed busy preparing for the service. A young man, every bit as handsome as Rocky, but perhaps a little older, hid a large machete behind the floor-length drapes.

"That's my brother," Rocky said. The room had started to grow hushed.

"What's the machete for?" I said.

"There's a goat in the back that will be sacrificed if things go right. People are starting to sit down. Let's find a seat."

A goat in the back, I thought, that will be sacrificed if things go right? What kind of "things," I wondered.

About 25 old wooden folding chairs formed an open-ended circle in the room. Everybody was to have a front-row seat. We found two chairs together about in the center of the circle. The Spanish-whispered chatter ended. A young girl of about 16, again dressed in white, brought in a clear glass bowl filled with water. Flower petals floated in it. She set it on the table and sat down. I thought of Vestal Virgins. There were three empty chairs near the table. One of the doors opened and a middle-aged man and woman helped a hobbling old woman with a cane to one of the empty chairs. All three sat down.

"That's my grandmother," Rocky whispered very close to my ear. His warm breath made the hairs on the back of my neck stand up. Another part of my anatomy was getting the same idea.

A low Spanish chant slowly filled the room. The young virgin picked up the water bowl of petals and moved around the circle as she dipped her finger tips in the water and, like a priestess, flicked it on each person, as she made her way around the circle. When she came to me, she hesitated for a very fraction of a second. I saw Rocky give a nearly imperceptible nod, just before she anointed me too. When she was finished she sat down.

The middle-aged man who had escorted Rocky's grandmother into the room, retrieved the cigar from the table. He didn't smell it, or crinkle it between his fingers near his ear, as I have seen many cigar smokers do. He didn't trim the end with tiny special scissors. He simply lit it with a large wooden match he scratched on the end of his thumbnail.

Once lit, he passed it to Rocky's grandmother. She inhaled deeply and passed it down the line. Each in turn inhaled the strong tobacco smoke. When it was my turn, I was glad I had practiced smoking cigars. It had preceded a special interlude in The Other Room on Clementina. I French inhaled. No cough. Show off, I thought. I passed the cigar along to Rocky. I exhaled, remembering my previous cigar session. Sometimes a cigar is just a cigar. But then sometimes it isn't.

Next came the rum bottle. It too made the rounds of the circle. Most took tiny sips, reminiscent of consecrated wine from a communal cup. Others gulped thirstily from the bottle. More

Spanish chanting now of an individual nature.

Suddenly, the young girl who had anointed us with the flower water gave a high-pitched Spanish trill, spun around a few times in the center of the circle as if she were a misplaced ballerina from a Degas painting, and collapsed in an artful heap on the maple floor. As if one, three young men in white, who looked like they could be cousins, leapt from their folding chairs and covered her body with theirs, in a parody of a multi-headed two-backed beast. Lucky girl.

"What's happening?" I whispered to Rocky. I felt I was watching an opera and didn't know the score.

"A dark spirit entered her. They are driving it away."

The girl seemed to come out of her trance. She sat up on the floor, and looked at the three young men. It no longer seemed decorous for them to be in such an intimate pile on the floor. Too bad. They all returned to their folding chairs. Low Spanish chanting resumed. I felt I should applaud. I didn't.

Suddenly a deep profundo voice boomed across the room. All fell silent.

"That's my grandfather," Rocky whispered, again very close to my ear. Again I experienced the same results from his warm breath in my ear.

I looked around the room to see where the grandfather was. Again the deep voice spoke in Spanish. I had no idea what it said, but was it possible? The deep male voice seemed to come from Rocky's grandmother. I looked at Rocky with raised eyebrows in a silent question mark.

"He's speaking through my grandmother," he whispered.

"What's he saying?" I asked. This time my lips were very close to Rocky's ear.

"He says the dark one in the room must be cleansed."

I looked around the room. "Who's that?" I said, nearly putting my tongue in his ear.

"He means you," Rocky said.

There was much Spanish whispering in the room. Why hadn't I taken Spanish, I thought, in a sudden panic. What good were Latin and French now?

"He's calling for you," Rocky said, in a normal tone.

"But I don't know Spanish," I said, as I looked toward the floor-length drapes. I couldn't tell if the machete was still behind them. Sweat trickled down my back.

"I'll translate," he said, as we both walked toward his grandmother.

I squatted rather than knelt in front of the old lady. Her dusky face wore a set of wrinkles like a fine mask of Georgia O'Keeffe. She spoke in her old-lady voice again. Rocky no longer whispered but told me quietly what she said.

I had three friends, she told me, who were false friends. They meant me harm. She would give me power to protect myself. This came out in short Spanish sentences that Rocky translated in what seemed a very formal and old-fashioned way. The advice was interspersed with sips from the rum bottle. First she would sip and then offer the bottle to me and I would sip. Then she took a small "dead" cigar from her pocket. Some more Spanish. Her voice was the only sound in the room.

"She needs something red from you. A red ribbon to tie around the cigar," Rocky told me.

A red ribbon, I thought. Not exactly stock-in-trade for a South of Market leatherman. I did have something red, however. I pulled a handkerchief from my left rear pocket. Very carefully I tore a narrow strip from along its edge and placed it in the old woman's hand. It was wrapped deftly three times around the cigar stub and tied in a knot. She lit the cigar, inhaled, and passed it to me. This time I did not show off. I merely inhaled. This was repeated three times. It was alternated with sips of rum. Finally, Grandmother put the still-lit cigar stub backwards into her toothless mouth. She took it out again. It was no longer lit. She placed it in my right palm and closed my fingers around it. She patted my hand, as if to say that everything would be all right. The cigar was not even warm. While she was doing this, she kept speaking in Spanish. Rocky kept translating, phrase by phrase, almost as quickly as she spoke. He could have worked at the United Nations.

"She says that if you ever find yourself in trouble, if you ever need help, just 'turn on' the cigar, think of her, and she will be there to help you."

"Turn on the cigar?"

"Light it," he said, as if it were the most obvious thing in the world.

The ritual ended shortly after my salvation. I was embraced by Rocky and several of the young women. They were all very chaste embraces. They reminded me of church-women embraces I received the summer I was 11, when I found salvation in the baptismal waters of Bass Lake. Neither time did handsome young men embrace me. Just as I was leaving, I saw Rocky's brother remove the machete from behind the drapes and head toward the back door.

When I left the Santeria ceremony I headed for John's place, to help celebrate his 40th birthday. A large Klieg light swept the sky as I neared Church Street, a couple of blocks west of Guerrero. As I got closer I realized the Klieg was parked in front of John's house. Of course, I thought. It was searching for secrets, in hidden places, known only to the cognoscenti of San Francisco.

The convivial rumble and chatter of a crowd enjoying itself greeted me as I ascended the outer steps of the Edwardian townhouse. A high-pitched laugh pierced the air.

I knocked, but doubted anyone could hear me above the din of good times. I opened the heavy paneled door, stepped in, and looked around. An all-male cocktail party was in full swing. I spotted Bill Essex. He wore no shirt, the better to show off his bodybuilder physique. He headed my way.

"The bar's over this way," he shouted.

I followed him through the crowd to one end of the long living room, where a temporary bar was set up.

"What'll you have, sir?" the young bartender said, with a slightly British accent. Did he speak Empire too, I wondered. He too wore no shirt.

"Gin and tonic," I told him, "with lots of ice." I didn't want a tepid English gin and tonic. He had a swimmer's build. I noticed his long graceful hands, as he gave me my gin and a sly smile.

There was plenty of ice, and an unspoken promise of more.

"You've never been here before," Bill said. "Let me give you the grand tour."

I got the grand tour. I could have been in a London townhouse. The elegant interior contrasted well with the shabby chic of the exterior.

"The exterior's meant to discourage cat burglars," Bill said, as if reading my mind.

As we came out of "Sister Anne's Room," Bill pulled me into the bathroom off the upstairs hallway. An antique clawfoot bathtub, the exterior painted forest green, sat at an angle in a large room filled with tropical plants. Potted palms and hanging ferns gave the feel of a private conservatory. Multi-mullioned French doors led to a private roof deck. It was not for a quickie, but for a snort, that Bill had dragged me in there.

"I need to freshen my drink," I told Bill, as we came down the stairs.

"The bartender's name's Mike," Bill said. "I should have introduced you."

Sharp.

"John was receiving in the library, the last I knew," Bill added, as he headed for the front door. Another guest had just arrived.

I entered the library to give my congratulations to John for reaching his 40th. There was a marble bust of a youth on his desk.

"That's an exquisite *puer*, John. Where did you get it?"

"An old friend of mine, in London, gave it to me the last time I was there. It's from Roman Britain."

"Do you know who it is?"

"It's thought to be Antinous, Hadrian's lover. He drowned while still a youth. The emperor deified him."

A little after midnight, I left John's place with Mike the bartender's phone number, and headed back South of Market.

Sometime later, during the waning months of the Leatherneck bar, Rocky arrived at work one night driving a new red MG. He told Allan he was quitting his job. His new lover, a doctor in

Marin County, didn't want him getting home so late. The bar closed at 2:30 in the morning. The new MG had convinced Rocky his future lay in Marin County, not on Folsom Street.

Chasing Film

Like Rome, San Francisco is a city of hills. Nob Hill is crowned with jewels, such as Grace Episcopal Cathedral and the Fairmont Hotel. Not far away was another jewel, the Nob Hill Cinema. Opened by Cliff Newman, it was the City's gay-porn star. I hadn't been in the City long before I decided to check out Newman's Nob Hill.

Lady-Parking-Luck was with me. I maneuvered my pickup truck into a space on Bush Street, less than a block from the Nob Hill. I hoped another Poole classic such as *Bijou* might be playing. The old marquee out over the sidewalk said no-such-luck. I paid my money and went in. As soon as I entered the small auditorium I knew what the feature was. The triple-X action by naked men up on the big screen was not the main attraction. It was a catalyst. The critical mass of men cruising the aisles was the main event.

I saw a passage to a room behind the screen. I entered that room and saw men come and go, looking for Michelangelo's David. I had a follower. A young Castro-ite with mustache, crotch-worn Levi's, work boots, and plaid shirt had followed me into the back room. I ducked into an empty open alcove. Within seconds the young lumberjack was down on his knees in front of me, fumbling with my fly. Seconds later, I saw Mr. Toad. He too had sidled into the alcove and was about to get on his knees. I knew this would not work.

"Back up six feet!" I ordered. With my brown leather motorcycle jacket and close-cropped hair and beard, I projected an aura of authority. My young friend from the Castro looked up at me. My eyes said stay. Mr. Toad knew the order was for him. He backed up five feet and rubbed his crotch.

"Another foot," I ordered.

He backed up another foot.

"Get that cock out!" I commanded. "Now!"

Mr. Toad pulled his zipper down and his meat out. It was a large, handsome, uncut cock. At the same time, the lumberjack pulled out my equipment and went down on it. Mr. Toad started to jack off, watching the blow job. This was terrific.

"Did I tell you to jerk off?"

"No sir!"

"Stop!" I ordered. He quit jacking off. I waited a minute while Mr. Castro worked on my tool. He had his own cock out now and was stroking it to the rhythm of the blow job he gave.

"Start!" I ordered Mr. Toad. He started jacking off again.

Between "stop" and "start" I soon had all in sync. It was like calling out cadence for my college ROTC drill sergeant.

Mr. Toad came first. Then Mr. Castro made his deposit at my feet. I let out a rebel yell and released my load. I like this theater, I thought. I'll be back.

The summer I was 17, I ran away to Milwaukee for the weekend. I saw Hitchcock's *Psycho.* I saw Fellini's *La Dolce Vita.* I knew these were not movies. They were films. I was bitten by the film bug. Back in the day, before videos and DVDs, before the Internet, before Netflix, film buffs went to foreign and art film theaters. In most cities they were scarce. Not so in San Francisco.

San Francisco in the 1970s was the gay man's paradise, the leatherman's Valhalla, and the Elysian Fields for film aficionados.

One Sunday afternoon, soon after I moved to the City, Jack Fritscher packed four of us into his Toyota Land Cruiser. We headed for the Lumiere Theatre, at California and Polk, to see the work of Alejandro Jodorowsky. It was a double feature: *El Topo* and *The Holy Mountain.* Jack had told me about this Russian Jewish director, born in Chile, who worked in Paris and Mexico, but I had never seen any of his work before.

Jodorowsky, along with Fernando Arrabal from Spain and the French surrealist Roland Topor, were instrumental in initiating an artistic movement referred to as *El Panico. Panic!* It centered on terror and humor simultaneously. It alluded to the great god Pan.

"Why didn't we get crowds like this at our film fests?" I asked while we waited in the packed lobby of the Lumiere. Jack Fritscher and I had collaborated on our own film fests in a Great Lakes college town BSF: Before San Francisco.

"You didn't wear leather," Jack quipped. The crowd, nearly all male, was overwhelmingly skewed toward leather. You could smell it. From the leather vests to the Levi's with chaps, it smelled male.

El Topo, a Zen-surreal-spaghetti western, takes the viewer beyond the most vivid imagination of any early Eastwood. The scene of the Colonel's collection of testicles in formaldehyde is not for the faint of heart. The second feature, *The Holy Mountain*, leads the cast through a series of scenes of ritual death and rebirth. The excrement of a thief is transformed by an alchemist into gold.

The cast journeys to Lotus Island for the secret of immortality; all ascend the holy mountain to confront their worst fears. *El Panico!* The immortals are shown to be faceless mannequins. We, the audience, see cameras, lights, and the film crew lurking just to the side of the film set. All are told to leave.

We left. Exhausted. Late that night, I migrated from reel to real at the Slot, a heavy-leather bathhouse on Folsom Street. I fisted two lovers simultaneously on the floor, while a military Minotaur squeezed their balls until they found the secret of immortality. Pan peeked in and then pranced on. San Francisco in the 1970s.

On 16th Street, near my bank, the Mission branch of Wells Fargo, was the Roxie Theatre. It was old and run-down. A small glass ticket cage was perched out by the sidewalk, where it would be easy to rob. The carpet inside stuck to the soles of your boots from decades of spilled drinks, popcorn and jujubes.

A five-dollar bill bought an annual membership. Films were 50 cents for members. It screened some of the hottest films in town. I walked by one evening and saw *Guernica Tree* on the sagging marquee that jutted over the sidewalk. I had seen Fernando Arrabal's *Viva la Muerte* but never his *L'arbre de Guernica*. I went in.

Guernica Tree, set during the Spanish Civil War, opens with

Count Cerralbo lecturing his black-sheep son Goya on the positive fine points of Franco and fascism. They share a glass of brandy in the baronial family library. While the old man lectures, young Goya masturbates into his crystal brandy snifter. He shoots his seed into the imported Cognac. He sets the snifter on his father's desk.

"What is that?" the Count asks in English subtitles across the bottom of the screen.

"That, Father, is a little bit of the only thing you ever gave me," Goya responds in subtitles.

Civil War in Spain during the late 1930s pitted fascist Francisco Franco and the Church against the Crown and the Spanish Republic. The film's anti-fascist imagery seems blasphemous to some. Arrabal allows his viewers to see scenes of anti-fascist forces smashing statues of Jesus, pissing on porcelain figurines of Christ, smearing semen on the lips of the Virgin Mother.

Dwarfs and midgets play roles in Arrabal's film, as they did in Spanish royal courts and Velasquez's paintings in the 17th century. Here they are neither companions for royal children nor clowns of the bullring. They are dressed as bulls and slaughtered in the ring by butchers disguised as *toreros* for the pleasure of Franco's gentry. Death in the afternoon.

Arrabal allows the viewer to peek at yet another scene: a naked child blithely playing in a room of human skulls.

I left the Roxie, stunned by the grotesque, surrealistic chaos of Arrabal's anti-war film. It brought to mind images of Buddhist monks torching themselves to stoical death and naked Vietnamese children running, screaming, in napalm pain. These images had recently played nightly on TV screens across America.

I got back to my flat on Clementina around midnight. Someone was lurking in the shadows of the stoop by my door.

"Can I help you?" I said in my deepest voice.

"Jim, it's Michael." Michael Monroe, the signature leatherman seen through the keyhole of my Keyhole Studios. The man pulling the logging chain from his ass. "Ready for the Catacombs?"

"Let's go up for a minute first." I had an idea. I unlocked the door and we headed up to my flat. The Catacombs was a very private club in the cellars of an old Victorian house at the edge of the Mission District. It was founded by Steve McEachern. You had to be invited there by a member. Michael had first invited me. If you passed muster, you might be invited back by Steve. I had been invited back.

In the kitchen, at the back of the flat, I got down two thrift-store brandy snifters from the top shelf of the built-in breakfront. I blew the dust off them. I got out a small bottle of Courvoisier I had been saving for a special occasion. I poured two fingers in each snifter. We sat facing each other, I, in a canvas director's chair, Michael on a leather ottoman I bought in Tangiers.

I told Michael of the encounter between Count Cerralbo and his son Goya in the Arrabal film. I took out my cock. So did Michael. I was getting a hard on. So was Michael. I dipped the head of my dick in the Courvoisier. So did Michael. We watched each other jack off and shoot in our brandies. We exchanged glasses, drank to each other's pleasure, snorted a couple of lines, took a Quaalude, and headed for the Catacombs.

That night at the Catacombs I thought again of Arrabal when Dennis, an ex-monk dwarf, slid his thalidomide arms deep into the bowels of willing penitents who floated on a crowded water-bed in the underground chambers. We emerged with Orpheus as the sun came up. San Francisco. 1970s.

Sometime later, at a Roxie Theatre matinee, I saw *Iphigenia*, the last of Michael Cacoyannis' trilogy on the Trojan War. The film opens with thousands of naked Greek soldiers wrestling and cavorting in mock-military movements on a sandy beach along the Aegean. They wait for war. The thousand ships the faithless Helen launched lie listless in the sea, waiting for the wind. Agamemnon and Clytemnestra's royal daughter, Iphigenia, must be sacrificed to raise the wind.

Cacoyannis employs a chorus of young Greek soldiers to advance the drama, rather than the traditional tragic women in black. It's breathtaking. The viewer sees the sacrificial knife meant for Iphigenia descend, but not her death. As in the ancient myths, the audience is left to speculate not only on her fate, but also on the personal sacrifices of all citizens vis-à-vis the state.

War was still very much on men's minds in the 1970s. Vietnamese boat people and refugees continued to stream into San Francisco.

When I left the Roxie it was still light. I drove out to Lands End for the rest of the afternoon. After following a rocky trail fraught with feral cats, I found the small patch of sandy beach in a little cove where men sunbathe nude. At first I thought I had the place to myself. I stripped and lay back on the coarse sand. It was then, when I was lying down, that I could see a naked man. He was only three or four feet from me, next to a depression in the sand. His eyes were closed. Rock outcroppings hid us from both the Pacific and the bay, but not from each other.

I lay down and, after a moment, I stretched out my arm to touch him casually, as if by accident. The second I touched his flesh I felt the iron grip of his fist pull my arm back behind me, flip me over on my belly, and straddle my back. I was pinned in the classic takedown I had been taught to avoid in high school wrestling class.

I struggled. Neither of us said a word. I could feel his weight along my back. From what I'd seen of him, before he'd pinned me, I knew he outweighed me by a good 20 pounds. I'd also seen he was uncut.

His forefathers must have traveled across time from Ithaca, on the shores of Ionia, to become fishermen by San Francisco Bay. His hands were rough and cracked. I felt his naturally lubricated cockhead enter. I struggled. A little. Then I relaxed into the inevitable as he bucked into my butt. I shot my wad along my belly pressed into the coarse cool sand.

I lay there panting lightly and stared out between two boulders. An aircraft carrier slid under the Golden Gate Bridge and headed for the open seas of the Pacific. It was the nuclear-powered *USS Enterprise.* It had been docked in Oakland. Had some Iphigenia been sacrificed so it could set sail to avenge an honor allegedly lost in the jungles of Vietnam?

I started to get up and realized I was no longer pinned down by Odysseus. I looked around. He was gone. I heard the engine of a small fishing boat putt-putting off into the bay. I put on my pants and left.

During that interim, between my sojourn with Jack Fritscher on 25th Street, and moving into the "dump" on Clementina Alley, I shared an apartment on Noe Street for a couple of months with Sheldon, from Brooklyn via L.A. The apartment was close to the Castro and cruising. Sometimes we both felt the need to get away from the neighborhood for a while.

"Want to see a movie tonight?" Sheldon said.

"Why not? Got anything in mind?" He did.

"There's a movie I saw in LaLa Land last fall. You wouldn't believe it."

"Where is it?"

"Out at the Surf."

The Surf Theatre was way out on Irving Street in The Avenues, not far from the beach. It was an independent art theater that served wine, espresso, and pastries. It was not easy to get there on public transportation. Sheldon had sold his car in L.A. before moving to the City. I, on the other hand, had Nelly Belle, my pickup.

"What's the film?"

"*Rocky Horror Picture Show.*"

"What's it about?"

"That's hard to say. You got to see it to believe it."

"Let's go."

When Sheldon and I pulled up by the Surf Theatre on a Tuesday night, the street parking was plentiful. We were the only ones in the auditorium. Evidently the film's reputation had not preceded it. It wasn't until it moved to the Strand Theater, on Market Street near the Tenderloin, and was shown at midnight, did *Rocky Horror* take on its cult status that swept across the nation.

The genre-blending film that mixed horror, musical comedy, and science fiction in a gender-bending sing-along had snuck into San Francisco by the back door. By the time I left the City, in the early 1980s, there were lines down Market Street waiting to get in. By then the audience wore costumes from the film, memorized the dialog, and shouted it out in the auditorium. Once, a schoolteacher waiting in line on the sidewalk was stabbed. Everybody applauded, thinking it was a skit from the film.

The Clay Theatre was another art cinema in the Surf Theatre Group. I saw Lina Wertmuller's *Seven Beauties* there. Wertmüller, a Swiss-Italian disciple of Federico Fellini, was the first female nominated for an Academy Award as director. *Seven Beauties* was Wertmuller's fourth film in which she used Giancarlo Giannini as her male lead. Set in Nazi Germany, Giannini plays Pasqualino, a handsome young Italian deserter. He's captured and sent to a German concentration camp, where he catches the eye of the fat female commandant of the camp, loosely based on Ilse Koch, known as "the Bitch of Buchenwald." Pasqualino tries to convince her he is too weak from starvation to have sex with her.

"First you eat," she tells him. "Then we fuck. No fuck, kaput."

He manages to survive. After the war Pasqualino returns to his Sicilian village to find that his seven sisters, fiancée, and mother have all also become prostitutes in order to survive.

Lina Wertmüller's next film, *A Night Full of Rain,* also starred Giannini, this time opposite Candice Bergen, in a love-hate relationship. Filmed in English, it is set in Rome and San Francisco. It opened not at an art house as her earlier works had, but at the Regency, a first-run theater on Sutter near Polk Street. Some had begun to suggest Wertmüller was less than cutting edge, while others saw her as a misogynist; her films as sexist.

A Night Full of Rain had a special screening at the Pacific Film Archives in Berkeley. Wertmüller herself would be there for a Q&A. I decided to take BART across the Bay to meet her. The place was packed. I was the only man in the auditorium. After the screening, Lina Wertmüller, in her trademark white-frame glasses, came on stage for the Q&A. Most of the questions came from a feminist point of view and sounded slightly hostile. Wertmüller held her own. Finally, when the program was ready to wrap up, Wertmuller stepped away from the podium, hesitant. She then stepped back again.

"Ladies," she said, "I have a surprise for you." She gestured stage left. Out onto the stage strode Giancarlo Giannini, exuding his dark Italian masculine charm.

The audience was silent. Then, from the back of the room,

a woman, with a Janis Joplin voice, belted out "Lina, where did you get that hunk!"

The Castro Theatre was the crown jewel of San Francisco's cinema world. On Castro Street, near 17th and Market, its large vertical neon sign announced *Castro*, welcoming the world to the gay ghetto as much as to the theater itself. The old theater looked like a movie palace should look. While watching the 1936 camp classic *San Francisco*, the audience would sing along with Jeanette McDonald and cheer on Clark Gable.

In late 1976 the Surf Theatre Group, under the management of Mel Novikoff, leased the Castro Theatre. In November they advertised for a new manager. I applied. So did Jack Fritscher. I had experience managing the thousand-seat Campus Theatre and organizing film festivals. Jack had taught film interpretation and organized his own film fests both on and off campus. One of us was bound to get the job. Neither did. The films at the Castro got even better, however, and the audiences grew. The Castro Theatre polished itself as an icon of the gay community.

Once I was standing in a long line at the Castro to get tickets for Rainer Fassbinder's *Fox and His Friends.* The line consisted mostly of young men in Levi's and Lacoste polo shirts sporting a tiny alligator. There was an elderly couple ahead of me in line. He wore a gray mustache and a wool herringbone three-piece suit that said "tenured professor." She had her gray hair in a bun and wore a double strand of pearls. Her boxy wool-tweed suit and sensible shoes suggested a research librarian. They were discussing film.

"What most people don't realize," she said, "is that in 1935 Hitchcock's *39 Steps* set the style for sophisticated banter between the sexes for decades."

"But the *best* scene," he said, "is where Robert Donat jumps off the train onto the Firth of Forth Bridge and escapes. It made my hair stand on end."

"What little you have," she teased, as she put her arm around his waist.

Just then a Pontiac Screaming Eagle Firebird pulled up and

stopped in front of the Castro Theatre. It was filled with teenage boys.

"Cocksucker!" they shouted out the open windows, then squealed their tires and were gone. The ticket line was silent.

"Oh dear," the elderly woman said, "I wonder if they were referring to me?"

The ticket line burst into laughter.

Fassbinder's *Fox*, although the main characters are gay, is more a film about working-class values versus upper-class values. It's a film about the exploitation of love. The couple portrayed happens to be gay. Some thought the film homophobic, some thought it too pessimistic. Most Fassbinder films offended somebody. It was New German Cinema.

If burgeoning Political Correctness was finding Lina Wertmüller not the feminist it had hoped she was, and the gay Rainer Werner Fassbinder not gay enough, Political Correctness was absolutely horrified by Pier Paolo Pasolini.

The Italian film director's battered body was found in Ostia, the ancient deserted seaport of Rome, in 1975. He had been murdered by a young male prostitute. Many thought the youth had not acted alone, and that Pasolini's murder was politically motivated.

Pasolini had enraged the Vatican in 1964, with his film *The Gospel According to St. Matthew.* He enraged the Church plus nearly everyone else with the last film he made, *Salo or the 120 Days of Sodom.* Based loosely on the work of the Marquis de Sade, but set in the Republic of Salo in northeastern Italy during the waning days of Mussolini, *Salo* is roughly filmed in four segments similar to those in Dante's *Inferno.*

Nine young men and nine young women are sadistically sexually exploited for the pleasure of their captors, the reigning men of power in Salo: the Duke, the Bishop, the Magistrate, and the President. One of the most egregious scenes involved the forced feeding of human feces. Elliot Stein, a freelance writer for *The Village Voice* and a friend of Luc's in New York, told me he had flown to Rome when *Salo* was being filmed to interview the young actors. He was curious if they felt "damaged" by the scatological scenes. While he chatted with them on the set, they continued to snack on the faux-feces of chocolate and nuts. Stein concluded they did not feel "damaged."

When first released, *Salo* was banned in most places throughout the world. In San Francisco the tiny Cento Cedar Cinema, near Geary and Polk Streets, had the courage to screen the film. To the shock of some viewers, they found themselves turned on by certain aspects of the sadistic sex scenes.

Paul Hatlestad, a friend of mine who saw *Salo* at the same time I did, returned from the lobby with popcorn and sat in the wrong row. Thinking he was sitting next to Steve Barnett, the man he came with, Paul reached over and placed a man's hand on his hardening cock to indicate he was turned on by the film. But it wasn't Steve's hand. Steve Barnett thought it was a great pickup move.

One night I picked up a man at Allan Lowery's Leatherneck Bar at 11th and Folsom. I brought him back to The Other Room. After we finished our fantasy—I forget now if it was Coach & Jock or Frat Boy & Pledge Master—we started talking film. Wakefield Poole's name came up.

"Have you ever seen any of Poole's films?" I asked.

"I sure have," Paul said.

"I've only seen *Boys in the Sand*," I said. "I'd love to see some of his other work, especially *Bijou* or even *Bible*." *Bijou*, starring Big-Dick Bill Harrison, had been critiqued as having a certain sexual *film noir* quality about it. *Wakefield Poole's Bible* was his only soft-core straight film.

"I might be able to arrange something," Paul said.

I wasn't quite sure what Paul meant. We exchanged phone numbers and drove down to Castro Street for early morning cocktails. We slipped into The Elephant Walk, a bar at 18th and Castro that had a beautiful large stained glass work over the bar. It was of a charging elephant, reminiscent of the Rock Hudson-Elizabeth Taylor film of the same name. It somehow survived the cops' revenge attack on the Castro during the White Night Riots. I found out later it was the work of Michael Palmer, my roommate for a while up at the Russian River.

It was close to two weeks before Paul called. We both had been busy.

"Would you like to come over Friday night to see a Wakefield Poole film?" he said.

"Absolutely," I said. I had read about Wakefield Poole's films, read how this past-his-prime ballet dancer had moved behind the camera and turned gay porn into art-film-chic that even straights were lining up to see.

Paul gave me an address out on Fell by the Panhandle near Golden Gate Park. The place was the top two floors of a restored Victorian. To reach it you climbed a high narrow interior stairway past the first-floor apartment with its 15-foot ceilings. Paul was at the top of the long staircase. So were about 20 other hot men. I knew a few of them. Most I didn't.

"Wake's ready to start if everybody will come upstairs," Paul said. Had Paul meant Wake as in Wakefield Poole? He had. I grabbed a cold one from the kitchen sink loaded with ice and Olys and headed up the last flight of stairs to the attic screening room. I saw Allan Lowery and sat down on the floor next to him. The film was about to start. Allan held a small brown bottle up to his nose and inhaled deeply. Poppers, I thought. He handed me the bottle. Not poppers. Coke. Good coke. I maneuvered the small bottle to refill the special cap and snorted. I did it again. Once for each nostril. I handed the treasure back.

On the large screen I saw a handsome young man packing things into boxes. I knew that guy. I'd had him over for a session when I still lived on Noe Street. In fact, I had taken some self-portraits with my fist up his ass. It was Terry Weekly. The screen credits called him Tom Wright, but it was Terry. Near the end of the film, Peter Fisk, the hot actor with the tattooed forearms, pulled his arm and a stainless steel ball out of Terry/Tom's ass. Up on the screen, it rolled across the floor of the empty apartment and into the corner. We had just been treated to a private screening of Wakefield Poole's new film, *Moving.*

The lights came back on. Barely. Men had started to couple-up, or triple-up, recreating some of the scenes we had just watched on the screen. I found myself with a lithe young redheaded dancer from Eugene, Oregon, I had wanted for a long time. David's nipples were a perfect titty-pink, his ass a dusty rose. His freckled supple body could bend in any position I wanted it to.

I came back to the house on Fell Street. Several times. I finally met Wakefield Poole in person. He was Paul Hatlestad's lover. One night I saw all of Wakefield's films. There were just the two of us in his attic screening room. Fueled by Wake's free coke, the films went on forever. What a divine obsession. Wake would stop the film, we would each snort a couple of lines off an antique mirror, then he would tell me how he had shot the preceding scene.

Wake offered me work on *Mirrors*, a new film he was shooting. As carpenter, I made a three-panel folding screen for Mylar mirrors and rear-projection-screen inserts. Cal Culver, aka Casey Donovan, the star of *Boys in the Sand,* was filmed jacking off in front of the mirrors. Partway through the filming the mirrors were replaced with the rear-projection panels. Projected onto the panels was prefilmed footage of blond Lewis deVries, as Cal's chauffeur, jacking off. The Mylar mirrors didn't work the way Wake wanted.

As photographer, I shot stills of Cal Culver during the filming. I learned that Culver could go all night without losing his hard-on and then cum-on-demand. I also got to take home the white boxer shorts that Culver had worn during the filming. They proved a great turn-on prop in The Other Room. As a bonus, Lewis deVries agreed to a three-way at my place.

Unfortunately *Mirrors* was never released.

Two years of high school Latin did not prepare me for the film *Sebastiane.* The sound track was Latin. Fortunately Derek Jarman's version of Saint Sebastian's martyrdom-by-arrows had English subtitles. Artwork depicting the bound arrow-pierced nearly-naked body of the third-century saint has been the stuff of homoerotic fantasies for centuries. Not just in the West either.

Japanese author Yukio Mishima, in *Confessions of a Mask*, not only wrote of climaxing over a copy of a 17th-century Guido Reni depiction of the bound and pierced saint, but he also posed and was photographed as the saint himself.

Although the film caused riots in some cities, when it opened at the Cento Cedar in San Francisco it did not disappoint. The naked Roman soldiers with full-frontal nudity and erections were far superior to anything in the Hollywood gladiator genre of the 1950s. If you liked gladiator movies when you were young, you were in ecstasy over *Sebastiane.*

Shortly after Luc and I had seen *Sebastiane*, we were going through the Pink Section of the San Francisco *Chronicle* looking for a good film.

"Here's one,' Luc said. *Robert Gets His Nipple Pierced.*

"Can't imagine what that's about," I said. "Anything playing with it?"

"Yes!" Luc said, all excited now. "*Salome*!"

"Is that the John-the-Baptist's-head-on-a-platter Salome?" I said

"The very same. They're playing at the Art Institute up on Chestnut."

We were off.

Robert Gets His Nipple Pierced proved to be a short, hand-held camera documentary of Robert Mapplethorpe getting his nipple pierced. Definitely an underground experimental film.

"Who's Robert Mapplethorpe?" I whispered to Luc when it was over and they were switching projectors in the film department's screening room. We were seated on folding chairs. No popcorn. No jujubes. Not even espresso or seed cakes.

Luc shrugged. The main feature started.

Salome, a 1923 silent film, is an early art film shot in the United States. It is based on Oscar Wilde's play of the same name, a loose interpretation of John the Baptist and King Herod's daughter. The film sets matched the Aubrey Beardsley illustrations in the printed version of the play. Legend has it that the entire cast was either gay or bisexual.

At one point, as Salome approaches John the Baptist, the title for the silent action reads "Kiss me on the lips." The man of God refuses, and is sent off screen to lose his head. When his severed head is brought back on a silver charger, Salome lifts the lifeless head up by its hair and holds it next to her pussy. "Now kiss me on the lips" reads the title across the bottom of the screen.

Luc was in Paris, visiting his mother, when Jack Fritscher brought Robert Mapplethorpe to San Francisco. I first met Mapplethorpe with Jack at Gene Weber's place, thanks to Max Morales, a friend of Gene's. Later the same night, on a party circuit, Max and I ran into Jack and Robert at a big blowout in Wakefield Poole's attic. Who would have guessed this young Manhattanite-in-leather would become the heavyweight photographer who would soon scare the bejesus out of God's right-wing bullies?

Jim with Cigarette

1977: auto-photograph by Jim Stewart at 766 Clementina Street. Chuck Arnett, David Hurles, Bill Essex and others once lived in building across the street, seen out the window.

Beach Theater

We crossed the Golden Gate
While fog settled in to brood on
Left Coast bunkers that no longer
Guarded headlands in Marin

Alone we stood together
Then climbed down
The steep eroded path
To deserted beach below

The Bridge in fog again
We played the two-backed beast
Against a gnarled driftwood tree
Half buried in the sand

We heard applause
You stood and bowed
While I saluted to
The whistled cheers

A fishing boat
Had drifted near
The motor cut
To silence its approach

This will be shared
With beers and shots around
In some smoky coastal bistro
By Bodega Bay

Bill Essex

June 1976: Mount Tamalpais, photograph by Jim Stewart

The Naked Wine Thief

The Chalk Police would arrive on Clementina Street most weekday mornings between 9 and 11. The police scooter would slowly drive the wrong way down the one-way street. Using a long rod with chalk on the end, a mark was made on the bottom of a tire. In an hour unmoved vehicles were ticketed.

Retail shops in the 700 block of Clementina might have explained the "One Hour Parking: 9 a.m. to 5 p.m." signs. There were none. The street was one of small industries where shop owners or workers needed to park all day. It was home to those who could not afford the tony neighborhoods in other sections of San Francisco.

Clementina Street was "South of Market" long before real estate agents or gallery owners invented the term SoMa. SFO once called to say they found my lost luggage at the airport but they wouldn't deliver to that section of the City after dark.

"Chalk Police!" Bill Essex, a deputy sheriff, would call out as he got in his old yellow van and moved it to a vacant spot on the other side of the street. Bill was one of the first openly gay deputies hired by the County of San Francisco. He saw no conflict of interest in alerting his neighbors to the City of San Francisco Chalk Police.

"Chalk Police!" the owner of the small sandblasting operation across the street bellowed out. He came to work early once to sandblast some plate glass I found in the dump. It was perfect for the light table I was building from scrap lumber I found in the alley. The Sand Blaster slid his new Mercedes into the spot Bill had just left.

"Park here, park here," Mary, the artist from the Land of Enchantment called out, as she moved her sun-faded red Datsun with expired New Mexico plates to the space vacated by the

Mercedes. "I don't care how many tickets I get," Enchanted Mary said. "This old heap is still in my ex-husband's name. Let them haul it away, I don't need it, but somebody can use this space."

And so it went.

Joe Taylor moved into the first-floor flat under me shortly after Larry Beach, part-owner of the Balcony Bar on Market Street, had moved out. Larry moved in when the Gonzales's left. He had a deal with Clarence, the landlord. For a low rent, like mine, he was supposed to fix up the lower flat.

Larry thought he could convince his friends to stop by, and for the price of a good meal, they would work on his place. It didn't happen. The place was still a mess. Joe Taylor had the same deal with the landlord. The first thing Joe did was set up a leather craft shop in the front of the apartment. He was DBA Taylor of San Francisco. It fit right in with the other small businesses on Clementina Alley.

Here he made leather belts, cock rings, armbands, some wrist and ankle restraints, and the occasional braided cat-o'-nine-tails. These he sold at night in The Brig, a leather bar over on Folsom Street. Joe hoped to support himself this way. At the time it was not an altogether impossible dream. The rent on the flat was cheap. He sold his car for a small grubstake. The need of a car in the City was low. The demand in the City for leather fetish items was high.

Joe Taylor was from Tennessee, but had been working in South City for awhile. He quit his job because he felt hassled by the other workers. Joe was tall and lean, with a large dark mustache. He had a less than aggressive chin. There was a certain Scots-Irish Appalachian look about him that some guys found a turn-on.

Allan Lowery, owner of the Leatherneck bar on 11th Street and Folsom, was over to my place late one afternoon. Allan had grown up on a ranch in Wyoming and owned a Best Western Motel in the City. He sold it and opened the Leatherneck. At the time, he was my boss. I bartended at the back bar I had built for him. Allan and I were discussing the future of the Leatherneck over a few lines. We seemed to get our best ideas that way.

About five after five Joe pounded on my door.

"Come on up," I hollered out. "It's open."

When I was home during the day and not entertaining in The Other Room, or working in the darkroom, I always left the door unlocked. I was on the second floor. It saved a lot of steps. Joe came up and stuck his head in the door to the kitchen, in the back of the flat.

"Allan, don't you drive a green and white El Camino?" Joe said.

"Yeah," Allan said.

"Didn't you park it on 9th Street about 15 minutes ago?"

"Yeah. Why?" Allan said, standing up from the table.

"Well, they just towed it away. Don't you know you can't park there after five?"

"Why the hell didn't you tell me that 15 minutes ago when you saw me park there?" Allan looked ready to explode.

"I thought you already knew." Joe went back downstairs to his leather work.

"That's the same guy that came in the Leatherneck the other night and told Ron Clute, the bartender, that the cops had ticketed everybody parked outside after midnight. That the tow trucks were pulling up."

This had been outright police harassment. It had finally been resolved.

"Why doesn't he let people know right away when he sees something like that is about to happen, rather than after the fact?"

It was a rhetorical question.

"As far as I'm concerned," Allan said, "he's Bad News Joe."

He laid out more lines on the mirror for each of us to snort.

Robert Opel rented a storefront on Howard Street, the next major street to the north of my place on Clementina. We practically shared a back yard. He turned the storefront into Fey-Way Studios, an art gallery South of Market for gay artists. Robert Opel was putting on a one-man show of Chuck Arnett's work.

Arnett had hit the national press when *Life* magazine, in its June 26, 1964 issue, had featured his mural at the Tool Box, an early leather bar in the City. Arnett worked at the Ambush now, and lived right across the street from me in the same building as Bill Essex.

In preparation for the opening reception of the Chuck Arnett show, Robert Opel had bought a couple of cases of wine from the Dented Can grocery store a few blocks away. The bottles had Heitz Cellar labels from Napa County. They were packed in smart wooden boxes. It was good wine. Or at least it had been good wine. It had been stored in a warehouse that had a fire. The wine boxes survived but nobody knew for sure what the heat had done to the wine. The wine was a gamble. That was why it was sold at Dented Can for a very reasonable price. It would be perfect for an Arnett show in a South of Market gallery. The show was also a gamble.

One afternoon I decided to drive out to the Palace of the Legion of Honor near Lands End. There was an exhibit on rural Japanese product packaging that I wanted to see. The Pink Section of the *San Francisco Chronicle* had given the show a very favorable review. At the last minute I grabbed my camera. An outdoor sculpture of Laocoön and his sons wrestling serpents on the south end of the museum had once caught my eye. I wanted to get some good close-up shots of it as a foil for a photo set-up of nearly nude firemen wrestling with fire hoses.

As I left, I noticed the Sand Blaster's Mercedes was parked right in front of the house. Looked pretty snazzy there. My beat-up pickup was the other side of the street near Enchanted Mary's studio. I heard arguing coming from Bad News Joe's flat. What else was new? Like many of the places on Clementina, a steady stream of tough customers was usually coming or going. Most of what you heard was indoor street theater. It added an extra ambience of excitement and the thrill of danger to the place.

The Japanese packaging display was worth the trip out to Lands End. What especially caught my eye was how eggs were nestled in a net of raffia bondage and suspended at the market stall like a fishnet jock. Jack Fritscher had taught me the basics of Japanese body bondage after his 1975 trip to Tokyo. The egg cluster gave me fresh ideas. The exhibit program noted that most of these rustic methods of displaying goods were disappearing. Western concepts of marketing were spreading throughout rural Japan. What a shame.

The Pacific sun highlighted the Laocoön *pere-et-fils* in a sensuous way that was slightly menacing. Perfect. The sculptor of this copy of a Roman copy of the Greek *Laocoön Group* had thought a fig leaf belonged on such a public work of art. Too bad. I hoped I had captured the mood I sensed outside the neoclassical monument to the fallen soldiers of the Great War. I had used up my film trying.

Coming back from the Avenues, on Fulton, I hit the afternoon rush hour. I was about to turn off 9th Street onto Clementina to look for a parking space. A San Francisco paddy wagon was in front of me. To my surprise it turned down Clementina. I slowed to a crawl and tried to peer down the street beyond its bulk. The street was jammed with people. Some had locked arms to form a circle and were standing in the middle of the street. I thought I saw a naked man jumping up and down in the middle of the circle. Now what the hell?

There was no way through all that to a parking space. I looked at my watch. It was after five o'clock. I couldn't park on 9th Street or I'd be towed. I turned right onto Howard Street to circle the block. Once before, I had been able to back the wrong way down Clementina from 8th Street, to an empty parking space. I was in luck. There was an empty slot a quarter of the way down the block. It was in front of a burned-out warehouse. With the ease of a practiced urban parallel parker, I backed my pickup into the space.

As I headed down the street toward the crowd and the paddy wagon, I heard a police whistle. It was being blown repeatedly. The rhythm was not that of a policeman. It sounded more like a rape whistle, that erstwhile attempt to control crime in the City.

Two young cops, their muscles straining against their uniforms, were manhandling the naked whistle-blower toward the paddy wagon. The crowd had parted for the cops and their prisoner. Why was he still blowing his whistle? Did he think he was about to be raped by the cops? Dream on. Sweat glistened on his naked torso. What a shot. I brought my camera up to focus. Damn. No film. I had used it up on the stone bodies of Laocoön and his sons.

The prisoner was wrestled into the wagon and the doors locked. The crowd parted again to allow San Francisco's finest to leave with their booty. I started toward the house.

Bad News Joe was sitting on the stoop in a pair of well-worn Levis and a seen-better-days white T-shirt. He held his head in his hands and was shaking it side to side. I sat down on the stoop next to him.

"What's the bad news, Joe?"

"Look at that car." Joe was pointing to the Sand Blaster's Mercedes. The one I thought had looked so snazzy when I left a few hours ago. It was still where it had been parked this morning, after the visit from the Chalk Police. It didn't look so snazzy now. The roof was dented and slightly caved in. Like someone had been teaching horses to tap dance on top of it.

"OK, tell me the whole story," I said to Joe.

The whole story.

According to Joe, the whole story started back a few months before when I put a notice in the classified section of *The Advocate*. It had been time to expand my repertoire. "Master now accepting a few select patrons," it read. "Novitiates welcome." My specialty was not just belts and bondage, although sometimes they were included. My specialty was the fantasy trip. Indoor street theatre, if you will. Sometimes I moved the action to Ringold Alley, the after-hours hangout for anonymous sex; other times to the backroom or toilet of the latest leather bar in the Folsom. They were all places my patrons would never go on their own.

The fantasy depended on the patron. If he were a priest, I might lead him on a trip to the confessional within the confines of The Other Room. There he would, under duress, confess to breaking 11 of the Ten Commandments. Such a confession usually ended in a cathartic climax and a cleansing of the soul.

An opera singer who often visited liked to warm up his scales while being punched around with boxing gloves. Then, as I squeezed his balls harder and harder, his range went higher and higher. When I was doing my job right, he would become *Il Castrato* and sing soprano songs of Zerlina, the peasant girl in Mozart's *Don Giovanni.* At the precise moment he released his passion, the dog in the flat next door would howl in sympathy. My nightingale would get dressed and leave. His chauffeur, who had been waiting, double parked on Clementina, would whisk him away to his place in Pacific Heights.

Each session always started with a glass of wine in the front parlor, where the gas-log fire set the mood. The "tip" would be deposited in a large antique stoneware jar on the mantle. We would then move on to The Other Room and fantasies of the night.

Joe had gotten wind of what was going on in my flat above him. One night, during a Mr. Goodwrench fantasy, my patron was rolling across the quarry-tile floor on a mechanic's dolly. The clicking of the casters as it rolled over the grouted spacing between the tiles could be heard throughout the house. The next morning I ran into Joe as we both came out our front doors.

"What the hell were you doing up there last night?" he said. "Teaching horses to tap dance?"

"Something like that," I said. I explained to Joe how I was able to augment my income from photo sales, bar tips, and the occasional carpentry job.

Joe decided he could augment his income from leather craft in a similar way. Perhaps I should have explained to Joe a little better the cardinal rules of the trade. Once a patron has contacted you through your professional channels, always keep it on a professional level. See the "tip" up-front first. Never get personally involved. If they start to see you as anything other than a professional, break it off.

"So this guy answered my ad," Joe said.

"Yeah, go on," I said.

"Well, he called and came over last night. He was much younger than most of the guys that answer my ads. Great body!"

I thought I was starting to get the picture.

"Did you get the tip up-front?" I said.

"Well, not exactly. We got along real well, you know, and he said he was broke and just needed a place to crash, just for the night. So I kind of went along with it, you know."

"So, then what happened?"

"You got any beer?"

I did.

"Come on up."

This story was definitely going to be worth a couple of beers. I opened an Oly for each of us. Olympia beer was my favorite then.

As it turned, out Joe and his new-found friend had worn each other out in Joe's "room" the night before. About two in the morning they had gone out for a walk around the block and headed down Howard Street toward the Black 'n' Blue, the latest leather bar, for last call. On the way they passed Fey-Way Studios. The lights were on. Robert Opel and Chuck Arnett were hanging art work for the opening of Arnett's show the next night. Bad News Joe and The Kid went in. A few joints were passed. They forgot about last call at the Black 'n' Blue.

The next morning Joe realized The Kid wanted more than a place to spend one night. He started talking about getting his "stuff" from a locker at the bus station.

"In no uncertain terms I told him to leave, to get out."

"Did he?" I said.

"Well, yeah, kind of, but he came back."

"He came back?" I said. "Where had he been?"

"Well, that's when all the trouble really started, when he came back," Joe said.

It seems that when Joe kicked The Kid out, he went back to the only other place he'd been to since he had arrived at the bus station. Fey-Way Studios. The door was unlocked but nobody was there, at least not in the storefront gallery. Somebody might have been in the apartment in the back. The Kid spotted the two cases of Heitz Cellar wine for the opening of the Arnett show that night. A peace offering for Joe, The Kid thought. He heisted one of the wooden boxes and headed back to Clementina Street and

Joe's apartment.

When Joe's at his work bench making leather goods he leaves the door unlocked.

"Come on in," Joe hollered when The Kid kicked at the door.

"I got something for you," The Kid said to Joe. He set down the box of wine and stripped.

"He's standing there stark naked and then puts his boots back on," Joe said.

"Why would he do that?" I said.

"Well, I guess I told him last night that a naked man wearing nothing but combat boots really turns me on. I saw he was wearing the rape whistle I keep in the playroom. You know," Joe said, "just in case."

I nodded.

"Well, I pushed him out the door and locked it," Joe said.

"You pushed a naked man out your door?"

"I wasn't going to let him hustle me," Joe said.

"What happened?"

"I heard some loud noises and then somebody yelling and then that damn rape whistle. I peeked out the window. He was on top of that Mercedes that's been parked right out front. He was jumping up and down on its roof. He must have thought it was mine."

"Why would he think it was yours?"

"Well, when we got back this morning, a little after nine, it was parked right there. I said something about the garage had finished tuning up my car and brought it back. You know, as a joke."

Most of the rest of what happened I was beginning to put together.

The Sand Blaster had come out of his shop for a smoke and saw a naked man jumping up and down on the roof of his Mercedes. He was so surprised he couldn't think what to do. In his *basso profundo* he bellowed out "Chalk Police! Chalk Police!"

Folks came out to move their cars, a little surprised the Chalk Police would be there in the afternoon. When The Kid saw the crowd converging on the street, he jumped off the roof of the Mercedes and started to blow Joe's rape whistle. Still wearing nothing but his combat boots, he ran down the middle of the street. This was when the neighbors locked arms in a circle around him until the police could get there. Thinking he could shock them into letting him go, he started jacking off. That only caused the circle to tighten, as they were now determined to see the show to the very end.

I opened two more Olys.

Joe carried the box of Heitz Cellar wine back to Fey-Way Studios. The door was unlocked. Nobody was in the storefront gallery. Joe set the wine box on the counter next to the other one and left.

I attended the opening of Arnett's show that evening. He had a drawing I particularly liked. It was of a man pulling a large chain out of his ass. I had done a very similar photo of Mike Monroe, doing the same thing. We agreed to swap our interpretations of that particular fantasy.

Several of the Arnetts sold.

The Heitz Cellar wine was unaffected by the fire.

The gamble had paid off.

West Coast Beef

The canvas hung at the Ambush
Off Folsom Street

Sweet nubile naked Ariadne waits
As if on some ancient Grecian urn
While spike-haired strapping Theseus
And mesomorphous Minotaur
Duel for her with their dicks

BullMan's killed within the labyrinth
Splashed by some early SoMa artist
With bright polychrome Gauguin colors

Buffet is offered after for
Those who can't go home again

Beef tartare with
Capers onions and uncooked egg
A legacy of Baltic Russia when
Horsemen shredded red meat with knives and
Ate it raw

KEYHOLE STUDIOS'

HOT STUFF ETC.

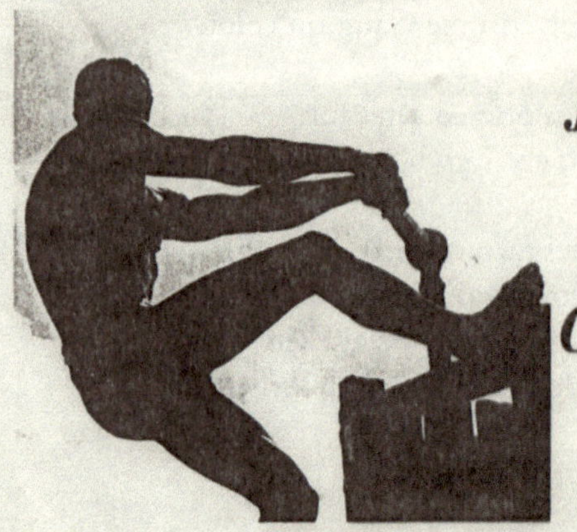

photos by
JIM STEWART
766
Clementina
OPEN STUDIO
12 - 5 p.m.
sats./suns. in
APRIL

Keyhole Studios' Hot Stuff Etc., Photos by Jim Stewart

Open Studio Gallery Invitation, April, 1977

Bad Boy Art South of Market

One afternoon I was developing prints in my darkroom. It was late 1977. I heard a knock downstairs on the outside door. It's a long flight of stairs, so I was in the habit of leaving the front door unlocked when I was home during the day. I would lock it when I was working in the darkroom. I finished spreading my prints of naked Bill Essex on Mount Tamalpais out to dry on the kitchen table and headed down. A handsome man, with dark hair and a trimmed beard, stood on my front stoop. He looked vaguely familiar, like someone I might have cruised in a bar South of Market.

"Are you Jim Stewart?"

I looked up and down Clementina Alley. "I might be..." He didn't look like a process server or an undercover vice cop, but then neither did Al Pacino in *Serpico*. Was he an old trick back to claim I gave him the clap?

"I'm Robert Opel."

"Then I'm Jim Stewart."

"I'm up from L.A."

"Why do I think I know you? Have we fucked?"

"I streaked the Academy Awards."

Ah. The light dawned. The Oscars. That's why he looked familiar. Robert Opel was iconic. Running naked in public during the 1970s had become a national craze. The bigger the audience, the greater the glory. Robert Opel streaked the live telecast of the 1974 Academy Awards just when host David Niven was about to introduce Elizabeth Taylor. That was a big coup. Niven had turned to the camera and quipped "the only laugh that man will probably ever get is for stripping and showing his shortcomings."

"I'm opening an art gallery here in the neighborhood," Opel said. "I need hot artists to hang."

At last, finally, and about time, opportunity was knocking! I'd had a show, *Men South of Market, Photos by Jim Stewart* at the Ambush Bar on Harrison Street in late 1976. John Embry, the shady owner of *Drummer* magazine, up on a scouting trip from L.A., had seen my photos at the Ambush. He approached me about publishing my work in upcoming *Drummer* issue Number 14. I agreed. Continuing the great tradition of starving artists, I would not be paid, but I would get a free ad layout for my Keyhole Studios. In that first decade after Stonewall, *Drummer* was new and touted as "America's Mag for the Macho Male." In the *mise en scene* of the sex comedy I was living on Clementina Alley, opportunity played knock-knock often on my door, offering sex, drugs and art.

As it happened, *Drummer* and Robert Opel, after both being busted in separate anti-gay incidents by the LAPD, were fleeing from right-wing oppression in L. A. Both were moving to the freedom of San Francisco to reinvent themselves. I went for the deal. In both my photo spread and the ad for Keyhole Studios, I listed my address as 768-A Clementina. That was an "underground" address I cobbled up by sawing a mail-drop slot in the gangway door that led to the building's unoccupied basement. My flat on the top floor was 766 Clementina.

Because the legality of my softcore porn business was still open to SFPD interpretation, I had hoped to throw off any vice cops with this little ruse. It hadn't thrown off Robert Opel, who had a nose for vice. Having seen my photos, he used his *Drummer* contacts to track me down.

I invited him in.

We headed upstairs and back to the kitchen. Robert peeked in the open door of my red-lit darkroom and inhaled the photo chemicals like poppers. The kitchen, a huge room the full width of the flat, had a big round table. There I'd spread out to dry dozens of newly printed five-by-seven naked pix of Bill Essex, early body builder extraordinaire and gay San Francisco deputy sheriff.

Robert Opel began inspecting his way around the table,

walking his fingers first. There was Bill Essex as quarterback, ready to score. There was Essex at bat. Essex the jock. Robert Opel grinned. "Stewart and Essex, Essex and Stewart. Regal, royal, rebellious. Doomed." He pulled his cock out. David Niven had been wrong. Robert Opel did not have shortcomings. As he pumped his way around the table he got bigger and harder.

By the time he made the full circuit of the table, talent scout Robert Opel had his deposit in hand. My Keyhole Studios had just passed the Robert Opel test. If art work made him cum, he'd hang it in his gallery.

"Do you think a hardcore leather art gallery can make it here, South of Market?" Robert Opel said.

"If not now, when? Gay bars are our only galleries. We struggle to be part of the art exhibits that change monthly at the Ambush bar over on 10th and Harrison. Chuck Arnett, Tom Hinde, and I have had some really hot shows over there. But it's still a bar, not an art gallery. We're ready for a full-blown leather art gallery. Gay art should get written up with real reviews, in publications like *Drummer*."

"Which I write for," Robert Opel said.

"I've seen your own photos, both inside and on *Drummer's* cover," I said.

"Is there any other showcasing for leather art here?"

I told Robert Opel about the new Open Studio movement, organized by the South of Market Artists Association. It encouraged artists to open their studios to the public once a year, on weekends. South of Market was just then beginning to be called SoMa, and Open Studio was mostly straight artists, but notices in the arty "Pink Section" of the *San Francisco Chronicle* lured the checkbooks and purses from Pacific Heights to the seedy side of the City. It let the polished side of the City go slumming in the afternoon, where gays played rough at night.

"Was your Open Studio show a success?" Robert said.

"Define *success*," I said. "It cost me. Open Studio makes each artist foot the bill. I called my show *Keyhole Studios' Hot Stuff Etc., Photos by Jim Stewart*. My flat was open to voyeurs on the weekends this past April. The straights who came by thought it was all about sex. They wanted the cheap thrill of 'dirty' pictures. The gays who came by thought it was about sex too, not art. They tried to wrangle an invitation into The Other Room."

"Sex sells," Robert Opel said. "Sex brings cash in through the door."

"Cash brings sex through the door." We both laughed. "I got exposure and experience from Open Studio, but my flat is not a real gallery. It's like self-publishing. We need a legit gallery."

Before Robert left that afternoon, I told him he should contact Jack Fritscher who was on the cusp of turning *Drummer* magazine from a little L.A. bar rag into an international leather and arts publication. Around his own kitchen table, Jack was recruiting and creating his *Drummer* salon of leather writers and photographers, and artists of all sorts, including Robert Mapplethorpe. This was ages before Mapplethorpe's work would get busted.

"I have Jack's number in my little black book."

It was to the advantage of the artists, the public, and Robert Opel himself, that Fey-Way Studios open, and that it succeed. I had remodeled my flat on Clementina and had been the design carpenter for the Leatherneck bar at 11th and Folsom. I pitched in, leading the unemployed construction crew of starving artists with grunt work at Robert Opel's storefront dump at 1287 Howard Street.

The storefront became a gallery, and the gallery became a salon that merged with the greater salon Jack Fritscher was creating around *Drummer* magazine. An invitation to an opening night at Fey-Way Studios was more sought after than a ticket to *Thaïs* with Beverly Sills at the San Francisco Opera. Get hung tonight at Fey-Way! Get published tomorrow in *Drummer*!

The inaugural show at Robert Opel's Fey-Way Studios, entitled *X: Pornographic Art*, opened with an invitation-only preview party on March 10, 1978. Fortunately my work had turned Opel's eye for this historic show, together with works by well-known artists such as San Francisco's Chuck Arnett, as well as Robert Mapplethorpe. Mapplethorpe was then an unknown to whom Jack Fritscher, once known as a religious seminarian, assigned a cover shoot for *Drummer* Number 24. It was Mapplethorpe's first cover and signaled the beginning of their infamous affair of sex and art that was seen as a scandal.

Over the next year, Robert Opel's shows displayed work by the famous, the infamous, and the unknown. Fey-Way Studios helped launch the homomasculine art movement in San Francisco's South of Market District. It was a catalyst, much as the 1913 Armory Show in New York was, when it helped launch the Modern Art Movement in America.

Within our own salon it was liberating, if less public. It was like Lytton Strachey liberating the Bloomsbury salonistas gathered in Virginia Woolf's parlor by pointing at a stain on her sister Vanessa's dress and saying simply, "Semen?"

Whatever it was, Robert Opel's Fey-Way Studios, amplified by Jack Fritscher's *Drummer*, changed the way gay art was perceived, valued, and reviewed by gay culture.

In the first 14 months that Robert Opel's Fey-Way Studios was open, there were two or three dozen leather artists showcased. Rex, The Hun, Domino, Etienne, Chuck Arnett, Robert Mapplethorpe, Tom Hinde, Olaf, Lou Rudolph, and others. Two shows, however, stand out in my mind.

Riding high in early 1979, Robert Opel gave me a card that read "TOM" across the top, followed by "Kindly Join Us..." The drawing was of a bare-chested man in full leathers, with his thumb stuck out; a hitchhiker you couldn't refuse.

Although this was the second West Coast showing of Tom of Finland's work, after Eons Gallery in L. A., Fey-Way Studios was packed. As a European artists made famous by mail-order and underground magazines, Tom of Finland had been an icon of the gay leather scene since the late 1950s. At age 59 this was his first trip to the States.

Seeing him across a crowded gallery was as much a thrill as first seeing some of his drawings in those little muscle magazines like *Tomorrow's Man, Mars,* and *Physique Pictorial* that featured black-and-white photos of guys in posing straps or a conveniently draped towel.

When I was in my teens, I'd buy those hot little rags that

preceded the gay press. I'd stuff them down the front of my pants, untuck my shirt to hang over them, and sneak past my folks to my room for a jack-off session. By the time the new issue was out, I had tired of the pix of all-American boys. I never tired of the grown men whom "twinkie-free" Tom of Finland drew. He gave us endlessly suggestive men as erotic cops, horny bikers, and heroic soldiers. He also depicted the villainous Nazis he had to deal with in his youth during the 1930s and '40s.

When I walked into Fey-Way Studios and saw Tom of Finland, I knew how Edward Carpenter must have felt when he first met Walt Whitman a century earlier. There he was. The man himself, the granddaddy of homoerotic leather art, signing his drawings for some of the hottest men in The City.

Speculation circulated throughout the gallery. Who would spend the night with Tom of Finland? Facing age 60, in the second decade of the youth culture, Tom was still a catch. My longtime pal, Max Morales, also defied time. He was in his early 40s, and made his living dancing a famous *pas de deux* with a woman in straight North Beach strip clubs. Max, who had modeled many times for my Nikon, sidled up to me and whispered "I'm going to take that man home."

I looked around the room at some of the handsome leathermen circling Tom. "I bet you do," I said. He did.

One can only wonder what the two masters with 100 years of experience between them did behind closed doors. Erotically, what does one do with the artist or the author who may not be the men he draws or the stories he tells? Secrets.

In all the sex, lies, and art of this drama that turned into a murder mystery, Robert Opel had wide and diverse tastes which he introduced to American gay culture. For instance, although Go Mishima of Tokyo was not at Fey-Way Studios in person, like Tom of Finland, he was represented by his rugged BDSM drawings of grown men. I had read the essays and fiction by Yukio Mishima, and felt my heart race when I read of his romantic, albeit right-wing, samurai suicide with his lover. I wondered how I had never seen the work of Go Mishima until I saw it at Robert Opel's Fey-Way Studios. I was stunned by my expanding horizon.

Like the oeuvre of Yukio Mishima, the paintings of Go Mishima, with rough homomasculine men in bondage, depicted the heartbeat of leather life South of Market. Like my own photos, his work jettisoned the pretty-boy principles of mainstream gay culture.

Most work at South of Market art shows, although offered at bargain-basement prices, was still beyond my budget. I was often able, at the end of the show, to trade my own work with an artist for work he had not sold. Since Go Mishima was in Japan, this option was not available to me.

There was one of his works I had to have. It was a naked young Japanese man with a gigantic hard-on. He wore a Marlon Brando motorcycle cap and was bound at the wrists to a pole. His teeth clutched a black leather jockstrap, and a pair of boxing gloves were tied together and slung over his erection. Was this "Japanese virility" bound by postwar American occupation? The price of this Bound Boxer was $375. That was over two months rent on Clementina Street. Nevertheless, I bought it and let sex pay for it by scheduling extra sessions in The Other Room. Pleasure for pleasure. The joy of collecting. And a fine investment.

Within our circle, Gregg Coates was a master of fine line art. He could take an ultra-fine-point Sharpie and create magic to carry you out of this world. I first met him when I was working for Allan Lowery, constructing his Leatherneck bar.

Gregg was designing the bar's logo. Part of Gregg's design was a jarhead Marine wearing aviator glasses, military cap and a dog collar. What made it interesting was that the word *Leatherneck* seemed to float from the dog collar like a leash. Was that word *Leatherneck* a pliable belt ready to come down on your bare ass? Or was it a strop ready to sharpen a straight razor before shaving your head? What was that at the end? Was it the end of a belt peeking through a buckle, or was it a tongue about to lick your dick? That erotic ambiguity was the magic of Gregg's art.

Gregg dropped by Clementina one night to talk about the upcoming South of Market Open Studio show that had been moved from April to October, 1978. We headed for the big round kitchen table at the back of my flat.

I got a couple of beers from my 1950s pink refrigerator. I never got around to painting it. The pink had grown on me and had become an inside joke about the weird irony of macho men who bought used appliances and became collectors of retro camp.

"Want a toot?" Gregg said.

I got out my beveled antique mirror and razor blade and laid them on the table. Gregg got out a new white bindle with a pale blue seal balancing a ball on its nose. He laid out four lines with the single-edged razor blade and handed me a short silver straw. I got to choose any two lines I wanted. They all looked the same to me. I snorted one up each nostril and handed the straw back to Gregg. He snorted the other two. With our fingers we cleaned the residue of our lines from the mirror and rubbed it on our gums.

"Ahh," we grinned in unison. As our gums grew numb, we each took a small sip of cold beer.

"So what's the deal on Open Studio next month," Gregg said. "Do I have to live South of Market?"

"Doesn't everyone who's anyone live South of Market? Here on lovely Clementina? Yeah. You have to be a denizen."

"Hmm." Gregg started to pull out his bindle again.

"No, no, my turn," I retrieved my own bindle from the little leather coin purse with the silver closure that had been my grandfather's. It was perfect to cart coke and its paraphernalia. I laid out four lines.

"I was wondering," Gregg said. I knew where he was headed.

"You know," I jumped the gun on him, "this place is big enough we could both have a show here. You could live here without living here. You could live inside my mail-drop slot in the gangway door."

"That would be great." I let Gregg pull out his bindle again.

By the time both bindles were empty and we were down to our last beers, we had planned our joint venture. Our two-man show would be titled *Double Exposure*. I would hang photos. Gregg would hang drawings.

Choosing my photos for this Open Studio show was a challenge. I decided to re-hang a few that had been in previous shows but to work them in with what became my basic themes for this show. Drugs. Bondage. Discipline.

Before Luc left for France, we had driven to The Geysers in Sonoma County, 50 miles north of the Golden Gate Bridge. During the 1960s the Geysers had been a destination hangout for hippies and gay men.

The Friday afternoon in August we arrived, the Geysers was deserted. We paid our small camping fee and hiked up the creek. We would frequently find small bath-water-warm pools in the stream bubbling down from the geysers. Before we reached the largest pool, we slipped on the wet rocks and dropped the jug wine. Our cheap *vin rouge*, meant to last the weekend, flowed in holy sanguination with the warm water of the geysers.

We stripped and bathed, hoping to cure with hippie gay geyser magic whatever maladies we felt at the time. Drugs and sex activate superstitious ritual within gay men. When we emerged, I luxuriously buckled padded restraints on Luc's wet wrists and ankles and pulled out my Nikon. I captured close-up water beads on his dark sinewy hands and feet, bound with broad black-leather bands. These photos formed the core around which I organized my Open Studio show that fall.

To these photos of Luc, I added four photos of Max Morales. They were all taken from the rear, to display Max's hot butt. The first, titled "Spring," showed that ass in open black-leather chaps and a broad-band leather body harness. The second, "Summer," displayed more of the same ass, as Max wore only a black-leather jockstrap. The "Autumn" photo repeated "Spring" with a black motorcycle jacket slung over Max's shoulder. The final photo, "Winter," caught Max in the leather skin of both chaps and jacket, displaying only the firm orbs of his ass. The photos were shot against a black background.

As an homage to Alphonse Mucha, whose art nouveau "The Seasons" had been so popular in the hippie 1960s, I published my "Mad about Max" series as advertising posters for the Leatherneck bar. They had never been offered as art photos.

There were other black-and-white high-contrast photos. I included a series of my neighbor from El Paso, his arms crisscrossed with black rawhide, self-injecting a needle of Nirvana. We were such bad boys then. Another photo I took at Paul Hatlestad's place. I shot a silver straw and rocks and lines of blow laid out on a black silk top-hat. Paul later placed the top-hat on the martyred Harvey Milk's casket when it lay in state at City Hall.

My *pièce de résistance* was a triptych in a brushed steel frame. The center panel was an ebony and silver crucifix, bound with black rawhide, shot against folds of black velvet. The two side panels, hinged to swing free, were both taken from a single negative reversed. It was a quarter profile shot of Rocky Ramirez, bound to a cross, against the black background bar-light of the Leatherneck. It was from the series of pix I had taken at the Leatherneck for a *Drummer* article on hot leather bars. I merely flipped the negative to create two malefactors facing each other. The triptych was the first to ring up the red "sold" sticker.

Gregg's fine-line drawings reflected variations on the same themes. One was a Pop Art drawing of a Hoover vacuum cleaner with a silver straw and razor blade titled "Super Sucker." Another was a continuous line drawing of three nuns with long straws ascending from their noses upwards to cumulus clouds titled "Heavenly Stash."

Over the next month, Gregg and I transformed my flat on Clementina into an ad hoc and credible art gallery. We moved all the furniture and things on the walls out of the double front living rooms, the front bedroom, and the hallway. They were crammed into either The Other Room or the big back kitchen. Only the black-leather tuxedo couch I bought on the cheap at Unclaimed Freight remained, in the bay window of the front room.

The walls, from wainscoting to ceiling, were repainted, covering the rectangular imprints of "ghosts of pictures past" left behind by the kind of tobacco patina more often found in French cafés. We installed a track strip of can-lights the length of the hallway. The old theater spotlights I had mounted on the ceilings of the double living rooms were perfect for gallery display.

Our invitation featured a shadow and ghost of a man pissing toward three toilets in the back of the Leatherneck. We invited in Max Morales, who set up his sound equipment in the overcrowded

Other Room, where he could build the intensity and tempo of the music as the crowd grew, and then bring it back down as closing time approached.

We hired a leatherman to impersonate a uniformed security guard, whom we posted at the bottom of the stairs to forestall any problems with party-crasher bullies. Joelle and two of her girlfriends agreed to handle sales. Allan Lowery donated beer and wine from the Leatherneck bar. Paul Hatlestad brought his handsome houseboy to tend bar. Filmmaker Wakefield Poole, fresh off his hits *Boys in the Sand* and *Bijou,* agreed to record the opening on his 35mm camera, complete with shoulder-mount sun-gun. We all wanted this show documented as evidence, for the South of Market Artists' Association, that what was happening here was more than dirty fag pictures for straight slummers to snicker at.

Less than a week before the show, Gregg and I were sitting on the living room floor assembling frames, polishing glass, and attaching photos and drawings to pre-cut mats. We hoped it all came together as the cutting-edge event we wanted to stage.

"Shall we have the last of the toot?" Gregg said. He slid my antique mirror with razor blade and silver straw across the carpet.

"Let's," I said. We had polished off my bindle over an hour before. Gregg laid out four fat lines of Bogotá's best. We took turns snorting lines and waited a minute or less for the euphoria to set in.

"Ahh," we both sighed at the same time.

"Back to work," Gregg said. He reached for the glass cleaner. "Out of glass cleaner," he said, as he held up the empty spray nozzle bottle. "Have any more?"

"I never clean my windows. I get more interesting light through them when they're dirty and streaked. The filth casts *film noir* shadows across naked bodies I shoot in the late afternoon sun."

The coke made this somehow sound very profound to us both. We sat in silence for a moment. Then funny. We both laughed.

"Do you have any more at home?" I said. Gregg had brought over the now empty bottle of glass cleaner from the all-male commune where he lived.

"Coke or glass cleaner," Gregg said.

"Either," I said.

"No. Neither," Gregg said.

"Any vinegar," I said.

"Vinegar?"

"Vinegar and newspaper clean glass better than glass cleaner." There was another pause.

"Do you have any?"

"No."

"What we really need is another bindle," I said, as I pulled out my wallet to check my cash supply. I was low. "I don't have enough."

"Let me see what I have."

We each snuffed our noses, gave long sighs, and laid out our money on the carpet, just as the coke was reaching its peak of perfection. We had just enough for another bindle.

"But what about the glass cleaner?" I said.

"When we're famous, and art critics and historians are writing about us, do you want them to say they spent their last dime on cocaine or on Windex?"

"I'll call Paul," I said. "Maybe he'll have some vinegar, too."

He did.

Opening night of the *Double Exposure* show was all we had hoped for. Both Gregg's fine-line drawings and my photos sold well. Some of the hottest men, movers and shakers in the leather culture South of Market showed up at the top of the stairs on Clementina Alley to add their macho sweat and talents to the inside street theater that our opening reception turned out to be.

There were just enough glitches to lend interest to the night. At one point, a young nerd-hippie showed up at the door. The uniformed "security guard" questioned the validity of his invitation. I was called down the stairs to straighten it out. He had been given the invitation by a friend of a friend of a friend. I invited him up. He got an eyeful and a hard-on. He had a beer before he went back to Berkeley, but showed up again at the public viewing the next day. He came back three times. He also came three times. Gregg and I saw to that.

In the small toilet-only room, I had laid out a mirror with a razor blade and straw on the back of the toilet tank below two framed pictures. One showed two naked Colt models tweaking each other's tits; the other was of two bare-breasted late 16th-century women; one pinches her sister's nipple while the other offers a ring. As the beer flowed, the line for the only toilet grew longer and longer down the hall.

"Stop sucking cock in there and get out. We all have to piss." The door slowly opened. Joelle and her two girlfriends squeezed out the door snorting up the last of the coke.

"We're not cocksuckers, honey, just pussy lickers," Joelle's younger tart cooed. The waiting piss-line burst out laughing.

We ran out of beer. Allan rushed off to the Leatherneck two blocks away to bring back more.

"You won't run out at the bar?" I said, when he returned.

"Hardly," Allan said, "Looks like you've hijacked all my customers!"

For the rest of October and the first weekend of November, Saturday and Sunday afternoons were open house for the temporary art gallery on Clementina. Saturdays were slow. Sundays turned into an at-home salon. Timmy Meeks, the houseboy I shared with Joe Taylor downstairs, answered the door, passed the hors d'oeuvres, and, in the small toilet room, pleasured anyone who was willing.

One afternoon twin Grace Jones clones with shaved heads joined the small group gathered on the floor around the leather tuxedo couch in the front room. A bald man in his 50s was talking, like animated charades, regarding the difference between art and pornography, between hardcore and softcore. "When you get to be my age," he said, "it's all soft."

"Like hell it is, Daddy," one of the Jones clones said.

"What's your name?" the other clone said.

"Doug."

The dark willowy twins flirted with Daddy Doug for the rest of the afternoon. They all seemed to enjoy the frolic they were giving each other. At five o'clock we closed for the day. I never saw the Jones clones again, but Daddy Doug became a good friend.

He told tales of life as a maturing leatherman; of trips to Greece, where dark Mediterranean hustlers took him for Mr. Daddy Dollars until, exhausted from pleasure, he told them he was an unemployed taxi driver who spent his last dime to reach Athens; of cheap rental rooms in the Zee Hotel on Eddy Street in San Francisco's Tenderloin, where he took hustler boys he picked up in front of Flagg Brothers' shoe store on Market Street.

He made senior sound sexy. I took glamour shots of Daddy Doug with his woven metal butcher's glove and my gambler's pistol, with his leather aviator's helmet and riding quirt. I wove them into my next show at the Ambush.

The *Double Exposure* reception was October 13, 1978.

On Halloween, October 31, 1978, I was building a catwalk for a fundraiser against the Briggs Initiative or Prop 6. If passed it would outlaw gays and gay supporters from working at any level in the California public schools. The fundraiser was in a large cavernous two-story building near the northeast corner of Castro and Market Street. It had an inside balcony across the back, from which I helped Wakefield Poole project various slide shows and a short film of Kate Smith singing *God Bless America*. Gays are patriotic and American.

The fundraiser was organized as a Second World War USO canteen. A dollar a dance, a dollar a cup of coffee. Red, white, and blue bunting and American flags decorated the hall. Some dressed as soldiers, some as 1940s pinup girls. The catwalk was for people to strut their stuff as they entered in Halloween drag. In the front corner was a tiny office where Harvey Milk had moved his Castro Camera shop. He didn't do much business there. He was busy at City Hall.

"Are you sure that thing's not going to collapse?" Harvey Milk said, as he nodded at my catwalk. He had just come into the building on his way to his new minuscule camera shop.

"It'll be fine," I said. I finished toenailing the support struts in place.

"Some of those queens are pretty hefty. The last thing we need is a disaster here," Harvey said.

"Everything's safe," I said.

On November 5, 1978, I closed the *Double Exposure* show.

On November 7, 1978, the Briggs Initiative was soundly defeated by the voters.

On November 18, 1978, over 900 followers of San Francisco-based cult leader Jim Jones' People's Temple committed mass suicide by drinking cyanide-laced Kool-Aid. Congressman Leo Ryan, who had flown to Jonestown, Guyana, the day before to investigate, was assassinated on the small airstrip by gunmen from Jonestown. So was most of his party, and the news cameraman who had accompanied him.

My pal, Mike McNamee, who was a TV cameraman, had been asked to fly to Jonestown with Congressman Ryan. Fortunately, Mike did not have a current passport. Another cameraman was assigned to the Congressman's investigative trip.

On November 27, 1978, Supervisor Harvey Milk and Mayor George Moscone were shot to death in city hall by ex-policeman, ex-fireman, ex-supervisor Dan White. Everything had not been safe.

Camille O'Grady Bell, Book, and Candle

1979: photo by Jim Stewart.

Camille O'Grady as Muse

Gay men often find women who add another facet to their lives. I first met Camille O'Grady on a cold January night in New York, before she moved to San Francisco. I was visiting Luc, who had decided to give New York a whirl after he returned from France. He introduced Camille and me at a leather *boite*, the Mineshaft.

Camille, dealing her gypsy cards, planned to follow friend Larry Hunt (a Robert Mapplethorpe model later murdered in L.A.), to San Francisco. Luc suggested a photo shoot once Camille was settled on the West Coast. She agreed. Over a year had passed and I still hadn't set up the shoot with her.

Camille had become to Robert Opel what Patti Smith was to Robert Mapplethorpe. She was crashing with Robert Opel in the living quarters behind Fey-Way Studios. Luc had given up on New York and was staying, for the time being, with me on Clementina.

I felt a tad uneasy approaching la grande Camille for a session. I wanted to use the shots I did of her in a one-man show the Ambush had offered me. I didn't want my approach to Camille, Queen of the Punks, to weaken my relationship with Robert Opel and his Fey-Way Studios. Luc had a solution.

"Camille is trying to establish herself on the West Coast as a singer, a poet, like Jim Morrison, whom she worships," he said. "You need to offer her a package she can't resist and let her sell it to Robert Opel, who considers himself her Svengali." Luc was often a study in *noir*.

"How do I do that?"

"Invite her over to Clementina. Tell her I'm staying here now. She and I haven't seen each other in over a year."

"Then what?"

"Buy a fifth of Southern Comfort. She loves Southern Comfort."

I bought a fifth of Southern Comfort. We all fucking loved Southern Comfort.

First we agreed the photos I took of Camille would be the foundation of my show at the Ambush. We also agreed that Larry Hunt would be allowed to shoot the setups I did of Camille, with his camera, for her personal publicity kit. Luc was uneasy with this, but I agreed.

It was also arranged for Camille to perform live in the Ambush at the opening reception of my photo show there. What sealed the deal was a three-by-four-foot close-up of Camille that would dominate the show. Since Robert Opel already had shows booked at his Fey-Way Studios into the summer of 1979, there was no problem.

The day of Camille's shoot my flat on Clementina was bedlam. I had draped heavy black velvet, once part of a theater curtain, both up the wall and onto the floor in a nook next to the fireplace. Here I could get smoky light from the streaked unwashed bay window, intense hot light from two theater spotlights mounted on the ceiling, as well as focused light from clip-spots on a tripod. Props were ready. Most I hadn't used before. They included a human skull I'd picked up at an occult shop on upper Divisadero Street near the Haight, a nickel-plated gambler's pistol that had belonged to my great-grandfather Thornton, a square bronze bell a friend of mine had cast in Colorado, an antique leather-bound edition of Byron's *Childe Harold* I'd found in a used bookstore on Clark Street in Chicago, and my grandmother Stewart's tall walnut candlestick, with beeswax dripping from a small stub of a candle.

They all would work as props for Camille's dark Irish beauty. Camille herself was busy expertly applying makeup with soft brushes as her multiple bracelets and necklaces jingled like the lifetime wealth of a Celtic gypsy. She was dragged out all in black, with a beautiful black silk fringed shawl from the 1920s of Isadora Duncan draped over her shoulders.

Larry Hunt, unaware he would later fall prey to a serial killer in L.A.'s Griffith Park, was busy tweaking his own camera equipment. He had been instructed to keep out of my way but could take as many shots of Camille as he liked.

Tom Hinde, a great artist whose work had been in shows both at the Ambush and Fey-Way Studios, suddenly showed up unannounced in full leathers. Tom and I had had sessions in The Other Room but never with a camera. Tom Hinde was a fuck-buddy of Jack Fritscher's as well as one of his Super-8 film models. Fritscher had dubbed Hinde a mystic. Tom wanted to watch me shoot. With a camera.

I could see this shooting session would go into part two and last all day. This was great. Luc was being especially helpful as my gofer. The phone rang.

"It's Joelle," Luc said, as he held out the long-corded receiver from the kitchen.

"I'll be right there," I said, as I headed down the hall. I hadn't seen Joelle for weeks but this was not a good time to chat.

"What am I up to?" I repeated into the receiver. "Well," I said, "I have this little *chanteuse* from Manhattan and I'm about to begin shooting some very San Francisco pictures of her."

"Better not let Camille hear you call her a little *chanteuse* or she might walk out on you," Luc whispered.

"What kind of pictures?" Joelle needled over the phone. "For feelthy postcards?"

"Yeah, feelthy pictures that predict her future. I'll leave the rest up to your imagination. Gotta go."

The photo session spun through a dozen rolls of film. Camille gave me everything she had and I harvested what I wanted. I was able to capture on film several high-contrast black-and-white shots of Camille with subtle allusions to mythology, religion, witchcraft, death, and a hidden hint of kinky sex. What more could I want from a single session? From a single model? Once Camille left, and Luc Alexandre and Larry Hunt headed out for beers, Tom Hinde and I initiated our session in The Other Room.

It started as a photo shoot setup with black-leather hood, motorcycle jacket, and open-crotch chaps with Tom's cock and balls posed atop two human skulls. This I captured on film.

Tactics and sensuality turned to cigarette burns and razor blades. This I did not capture on film.

A week later Tom gave me one of his new pencil sketches featuring red and blue scars when I gave him proof sheets of our session. I still have that Tom Hinde original. It exists in an ecstatic world beyond Tom of Finland and Go Mishima.

Opening night the Ambush was packed for Camille's performance. My photos of Camille and Daddy Doug sold well. It was the first time I featured a female model. The three-foot by four-foot closeup of "Camille as Atropos," the ancient Greek fate ready to cut your thread of life, remained unsold. Too *vagina dentata.*

Later that spring of 1979, Robert Opel came over to Clementina one afternoon. He was thinking of starting a magazine called *Cocksucker.* He wanted to know if I had any good photo illustrations for such a publication. I did. I pulled out some candid shots I had taken one Sunday afternoon when Sheldon Kovalski and I were fooling around in a secluded area of Golden Gate Park out near the Pacific.

Before we knew it, Robert Opel and I were fooling around. I pulled out my camera. Quite unintentionally we started an informal photo shoot Everything we did was art. He asked, almost wheedling me, about the human skull and nickel-plated gambler's pistol I'd used in the Camille shoot. I got them out. I captured a few shots of Robert fooling around with the pistol. Then I shot a few of Robert Opel, like Hamlet, contemplating the skull.

Little did I know to read the portents. Little did Robert Opel know that, less than a hundred days later, with Camille tied up on the floor at his side, he would be murdered. Assassinated. Shot to death in Fey-Way Studios. Camille would escape to go live underground.

Not too long after the photo session with Robert Opel, during that rainy winter, suddenly—I don't know why—I fled the vibes of Clementina Street, like Christopher Isherwood fleeing Berlin, fearing perhaps the speed trip, the speed trap of the 1970s, fleeing SoMa on instinct, and moved up to the Russian River, 69 miles north of San Francisco in Sonoma County.

I scored a job at the Russian River Lodge, remodeling tourist rooms. In the communal room one night, in May, on the 21st, we watched the news coverage of the "White Night Riots." This was the evening of the afternoon a minimal "manslaughter" sentence was handed down to ex-cop, ex-fireman and ex-supervisor Dan White for the assassination of Mayor Moscone and Supervisor Harvey Milk.

We watched as TV nightly news showed gays rioting in front of City Hall, six blocks from Clementina Street. Twelve cop cars were set ablaze. The rioters headed for Castro Street. The cops followed, removed their badges, and had their own riot, stomping down Castro Street, beating everyone in their path. The cops chased gay men, straight women, and anyone else they saw into bars, beating them over the tables, in the bathrooms, where 20 people were crammed, suffocating, into spaces meant for one.

A few days after the "White Night Riot," I got a call from Robert Opel. For a performance piece, he wanted to borrow, as a prop, the antique gambler's pistol I had used in the photo shoots of both him and Camille. I had no idea where it was since I had packed most of my stuff and put it in storage when I subleased my flat and ran to the River.

In response to the farcical trial of Dan White, Robert Opel announced to all and sundry that he was staging a mock execution of Dan White. It was to take place after the June 1979 Gay Pride Parade, in front of City Hall, where the "White Night Riot" had occurred. I myself did not see Robert Opel's performance piece where he, costumed as "gay Justice," shot "Dan White" to death.

Two weeks after the Gay Pride Parade, on the night of July 7, 1979, two men entered Fey-Way Studios and, in front of Camille O'Grady and Anthony Rogers, shot Robert Opel to death. Like Akira Kurosawa's 1950 film *Rashomon*, there was much freak-out and gossip over exactly what had happened. Robert Opel had been murdered, no doubt about that. Was it a political assassination or a drug deal gone wrong? Did it involve drug dealers or murder for hire? Or San Francisco cops? Who was behind it? The alleged killers were arrested, "escaped" and then picked up again.

Camille O'Grady and Anthony Rogers went underground.

Others fled the City, following in the stampede that had carried me out of town. Where gays were once safe, suddenly we no longer felt safe. American culture was in full tilt.

As in all good horror stories, sometime later I ran into Anthony Rogers at the Rusty Nail, a gay roadhouse near Forestville, on River Road. I took him home. We fucked. He stayed with me a few days in my cabin under the redwoods up Canyon One just outside the village of Rio Nido. Then one day he was gone. I never saw him again.

I saw Camille O'Grady only once again, briefly. I had crashed at some long forgotten trick's place on a quick trip down from the Russian River to the City, which took me back to Clementina Street and another man's flat.

In the morning, as we were having coffee and cigarettes, Camille emerged from behind a closed bedroom door wearing only a man's permanent-press blue button-down oxford-cloth shirt. She was like Venus rising from the semen. I wanted to reach for my camera but—bad artist!—I had left it up at the River.

Following her out of the bedroom was an extremely handsome naked man I had never seen before. He gave her a loud slap on the bare ass with his big hetero hand, as he kissed her.

"What a crack," Camille said.

"That's what I thought last night," he said.

She turned and kissed him back.

My three-by-four-foot blow-up of "Camille as Atropos," the Fate of Death, hung for awhile in the Balcony Bar on Market Street. It hung longer in a private collection on Kissling Street, three blocks from Clementina. Then it disappeared forever, as did much gay art during the AIDS holocaust of the 1980s and 1990s.

The 1979 loss of Robert Opel to an assassin's bullet was more than the loss of a friend, a member of the leather community, an inventive artist. Robert Opel's death also spelled the death of Fey-Way Studios, a showcase for homomasculine artistic endeavors, a part of the SoMa Salon Jack Fritscher continued to build through *Drummer.*

The loss of Robert Opel was emblematic of the loss the greater gay community was about to experience 12 months later when the fates suddenly caused our community to drop like flies.

Because of that art salon on Clementina, and because of all of us knowing one another's works, one of the shots I had taken of Robert Opel—when he and I were fooling jackanapes with my nickel-plated pistol, the skull, and my camera that spring day in 1979—became part of the Robert Opel legend. Jack Fritscher published my "Robert Opel with Skull" with Opel's obituary in *Drummer*, issue Number 31, 1979. It was seen around the world. It was a pictograph of the way we were. Of what once was.

Decades later, in 2010, the photos "Robert Opel with Skull" and "Camille O'Grady with Skull" were hung at SF Camerawork in "An Autobiography of the San Francisco Bay Area, Part 2: The Future Lasts Forever."

DOUBLE EXPOSURE

PHOTOS & DRAWINGS BY JIM STEWART AND GREGG COATES
• OPENING RECEPTION: FRIDAY, 13 OCTOBER 1978: 8:00-MIDNIGHT
• AUDIO BY MAX MORALES / INVITATION ADMITS TWO
• 766 CLEMENTINA ALLEY, SAN FRANCISCO, CA (S.O.M.)
• PUBLIC VIEWING: NOON-5 P.M. SATS & SUNS, 14 OCT.-5 NOV.

Three Toilets

"Double Exposure,"
Open Studio Gallery Invitation, October, 1978
photos by Jim Stewart, line drawings by Gregg Coates

Malefactors with Bound Crucifix

1977: model Rocky the Bartender

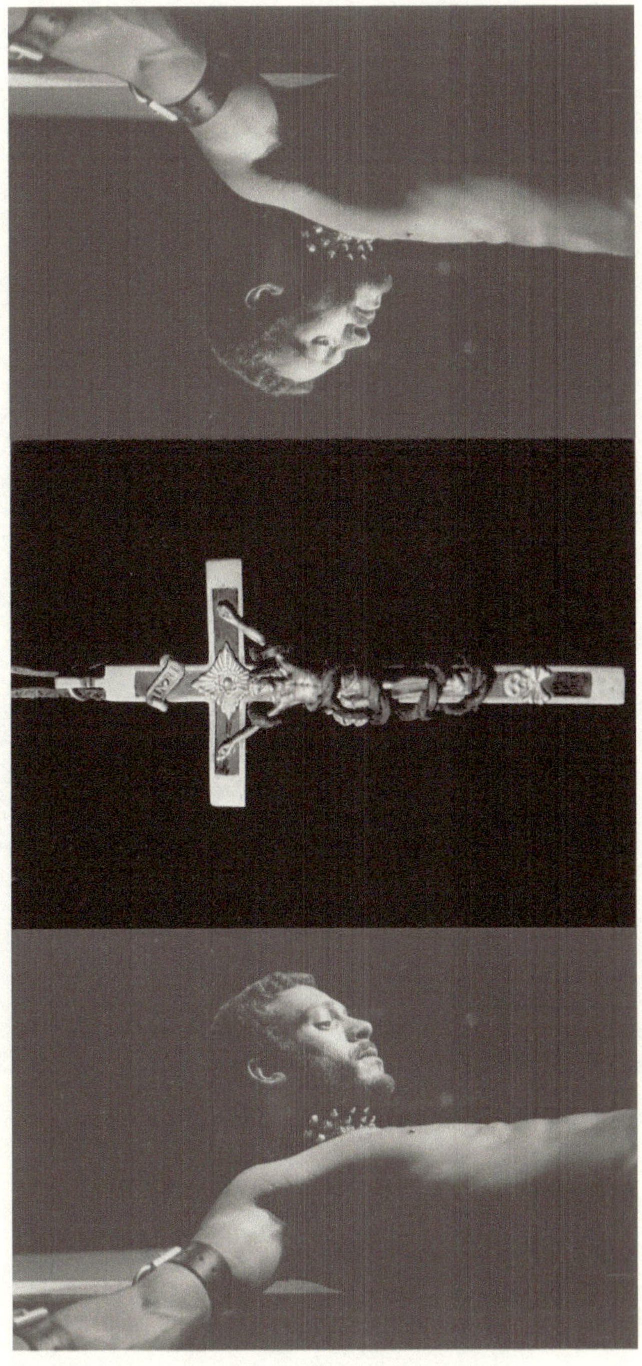

Jim Stewart Photos at The Ambush

Special Guest Performance: Camille O'Grady, 1979
Photo exhibition announcement

Camille O'Grady with Skull

1979: photo by Jim Stewart. Note: This photo was at the SF Camerawork in "Autobiography of the San Francisco Bay Area Part 2: The Future Lasts Forever" in 2010.

Dancer David Studach

1978: photo by Jim Stewart at 766 Clementina Street

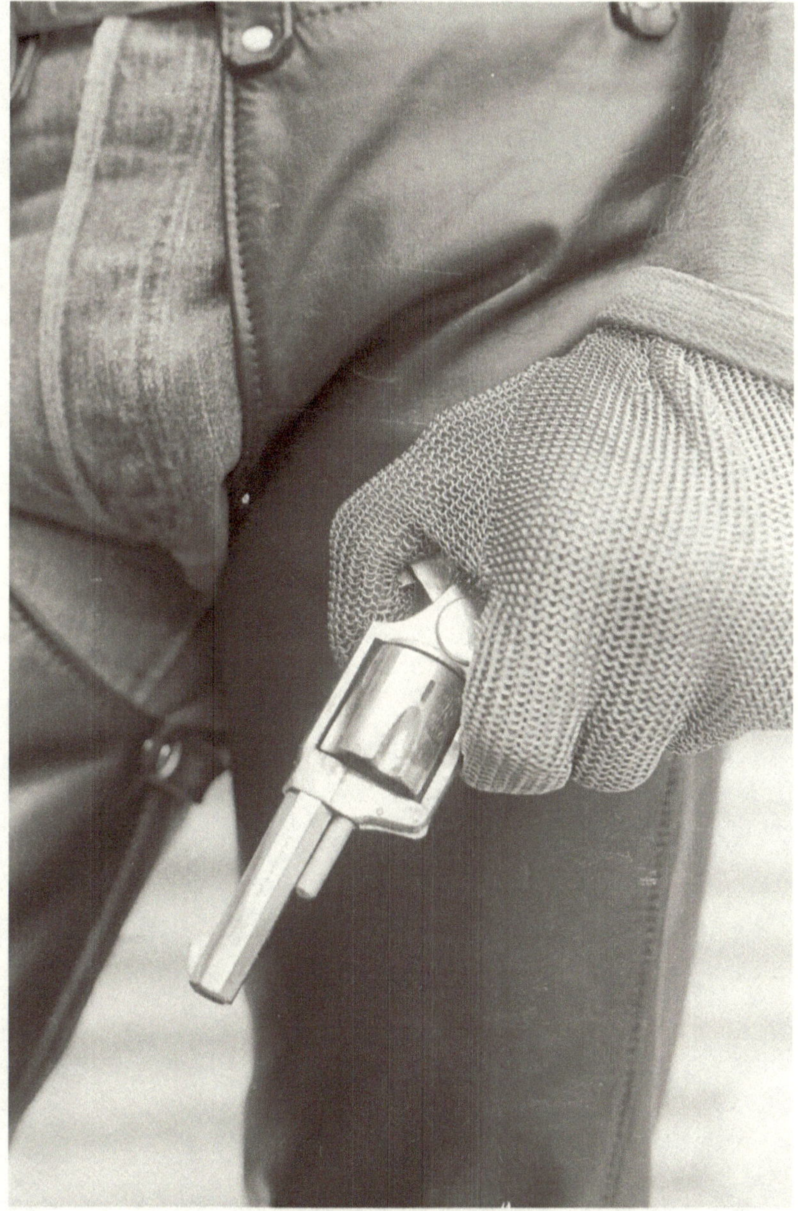

Daddy's Glove and Pistol

1979: photo by Jim Stewart of chain mail butcher's glove and nickel plated gambler's pistol

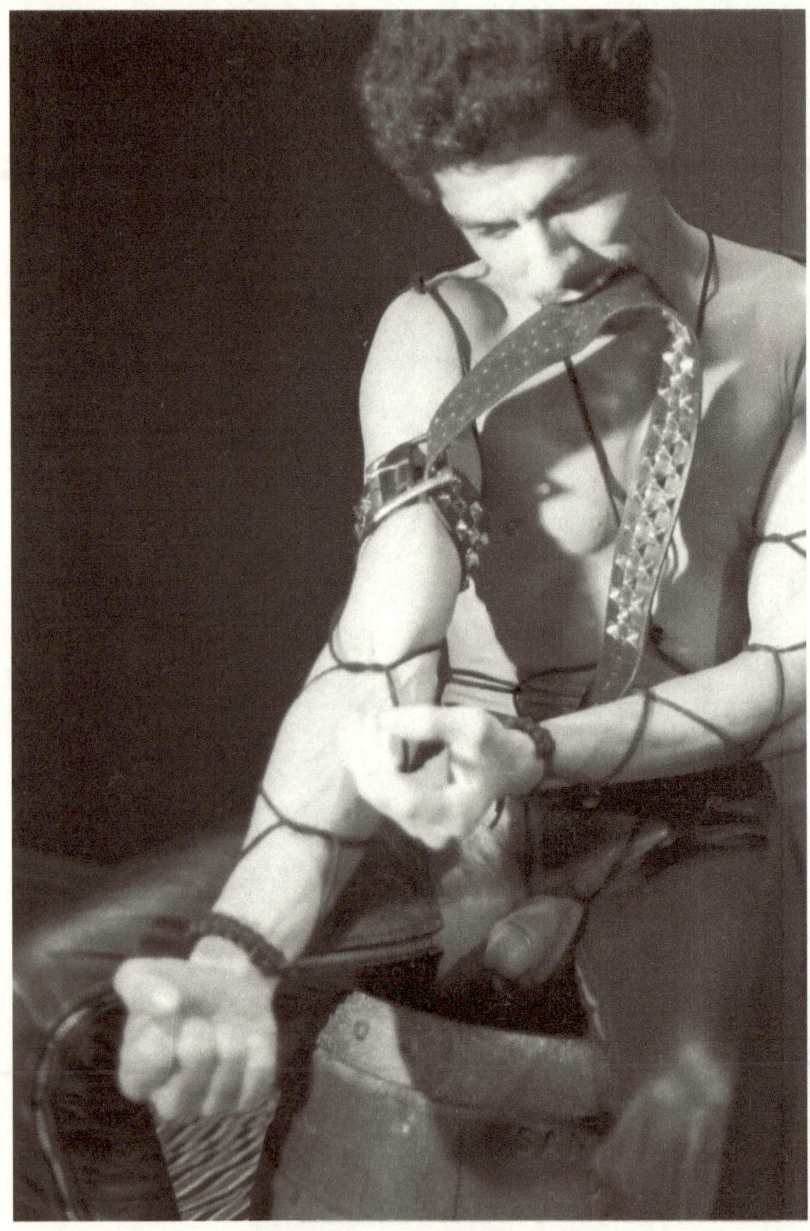

Drugs, Sex, and Leather

1979: model El Paso Ric, photo by Jim Stewart
in "The Other Room," Clementina Alley

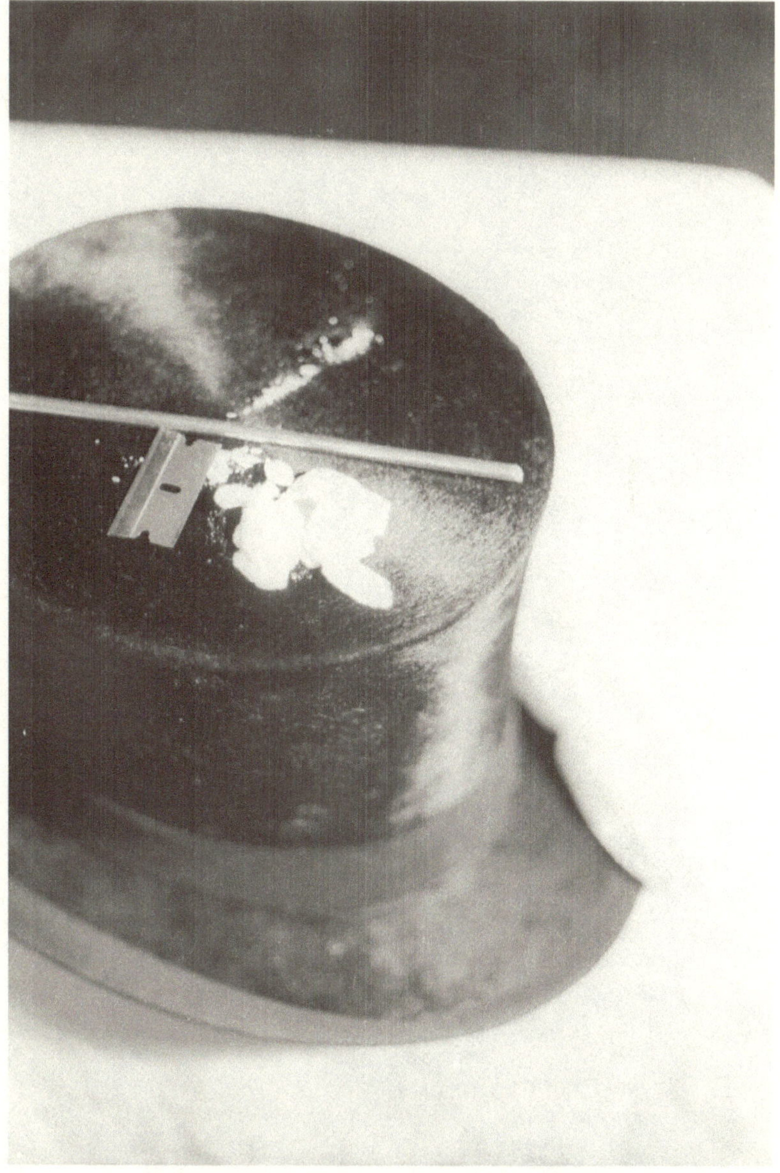

Putting on the Ritz: Top Hat and Blow

1978: photo by Jim Stewart. This top hat was placed by Paul Hatlestad on Harvey Milk's coffin when it lay in state at City Hall after his assassination by Dan White in November, 1978.

Robert Opel with Skull

1979: photo by Jim Stewart. Note: This photo was at the SF Camerawork in "Autobiography of the San Francisco Bay Area Part 2: The Future Lasts Forever" in 2010.

Up At The River

Everybody needs balance in their lives, between urban and rural. Sometimes the City can become overwhelming. The need to get back to nature asserts itself. I moved up to the River. The River referred to a seedy string of dilapidated resort towns along the Russian River. There were vineyards, redwoods and rednecks. Migrating gays, exiting San Francisco, were gentrifying the area.

In the spring of 1979, after the Camille show at the Ambush, I got a job at the Russian River Lodge on River Road in Sonoma County. It was a gay country campground with farmhouse rooms, cabins, and a pool for nude swimming. I would be the general handyman, remodel some of the cabins, fix up the rooms in the old farmhouse, and enjoy the sights around the pool when I wasn't busy. What a chance to get away from it all.

One afternoon we were building a redwood deck around the pool area. It seemed really hot. All of us were working without shirts. I checked the thermometer. It read 114 degrees. I consulted with Lee, the owner.

"Alright," I said. "We're knocking off early. Into the pool if you want." We all stripped naked and got in the pool. When I got out I dried off and headed for the house. My hair was still wet. I needed a haircut.

"Jaime," I said, "did you bring your clippers with you?" Jaime was a hairdresser who lived at the Russian River Lodge that summer. He lived naked except for his brown shorts and a tan nearly as dark. He sported gold hoop rings in both ears and both nipples. He brought to mind a chest of drawers by Salvador Dali.

"Got them right here," Jaime said. "Ready for a haircut?"

"Got that right," I said.

"Meet me on the front porch."

I met him on the front porch. I wore black, not-quite-bikini Speedos that I'd picked up in a bargain basement at some department store over a decade ago. I was ready for my haircut.

Jaime dragged out a 1950s kitchen chair, his clippers, and a soft barber's brush. No combs. This was going to be a short-short haircut. It didn't take long. As soon as I got up, Lee sat down.

"Give me the same," he said. Jaime gave him the same.

"Next," Bob the manager said. He sat down on the chrome and yellow plastic chair. The pile of hair on the porch floor was growing.

"Anybody else?" Jaime said.

"You might as well do me too," Wes said. I had found Wes sleeping on my front stoop on Clementina Street one morning. Joe, the leather worker who lived below me, thought he was a wino sleeping it off. Wes was the ex of an ex who hitched from Michigan to San Francisco to meet me. Wes took off his T-shirt and sat on the chrome chair. Off came his long hair. It joined the pile on the porch floor.

There we all stood, wearing various configurations of facial hair, but sporting nearly shaved heads like Nazi collaborators in liberated Paris.

The next day was rodeo day in Guerneville. Wes and I jumped in my pickup and drove into town. The sun was out. The thermometer hovered near 90. Not a cloud in the sky. The horse and rider parade started down Main Street at noon. We had our place on the crowded sidewalk by 11:30.

The bars were all open early. Drinks were served in paper cups so you could take them outside to watch the parade. Wes and I stood in front of the Rainbow Cattle Company, drinking Olympia draft beer.

The Cattle Company was a gay bar on Main Street. It was owned and operated by an ex L.A. cop and his partner. Some of the straight rowdies from the bar down the street used to hassle the gays when the bar first opened. That had pretty much settled down after the sheriff had been called in a few times.

"Have you picked out which one you want?" I said. Four young cowboys in rodeo shirts reined in their horses right in front of us. I lit up a Marlboro. Sweat stained the armpits of their fancy shirts. I focused my Nikon on a boot with elaborate leather tooling that the closest rider had stuck in his stirrup. Click. I was building a collection of Russian River wranglers. I took another swig of beer. A light breeze wafted the sweet smell of man sweat and horseshit our way." Which one I want?" Wes said.

"Yeah, which buckaroo you want to fuck the shit out of you?" I said.

Wes blushed. Or at least I thought he blushed. Then I realized he was sunburned. Especially on his nearly shaved head. "You better cover your head up, Wes, or you're going to have one hell of a burn."

"That's all right," he said. "I don't have anything to cover it up with."

I took off the Stetson I had picked up in Rawlins, Wyoming a few years ago on my way cross country to Jack Fritscher's place on 25th Street. I didn't wear it often, but it was a nice prop now and then. I plunked it down on Wes's red skull. "There," I said. "That ought to help."

"Thanks," Wes said. "What about you?"

"I still have a trick or two up my sleeve," I said. "Or rather in my hip pocket." I pulled a neatly folded dark blue hanky from my left hip pocket, shook it out, then tied it do-rag style around my own nearly naked skull.

"What's a blue hanky on a shaved head mean?" a gay *vaquero* shouted, as he whizzed behind me on roller skates.

"We'll have to wait and see," I shouted back, but he was gone.

"Get us a couple more beers," I said. I handed Wes some bills.

When he came out of the Cattle Company with our beers, I noticed Wes had rolled the brim of my hat to form a more elongated shape. It fit his head better. It looked hot. Gave him a little character. A little attitude.

We drove over to the sunburnt field next to the Russian River Rodeo grounds. Shirtless attendants signaled where to park. Clouds of dust rose in the hot afternoon air as beat-up pickup trucks, rundown vans, and used cars way past their prime pulled into the shade-less lot. The weathered wooden bleachers were packed. Horse trailers were unloaded at the far side of the arena. Rodeo cowboys and attendants gathered in knots on the early July afternoon.

Wes and I managed to squeeze onto the bleachers between a family with two kids dressed as cowboys and a middle-aged couple that looked bored. Sometime between the barrel races and the bucking bronco contest Wes left for the field toilets at the far end of the grounds. He was gone a long time. I maneuvered through the crowd and up as close to the arena as the public was allowed. I was getting some great shots for my River wrangler collection. Wes finally came back.

"I got a ride," he said. He looked down at the dust by the end of the bleachers where I stood in the shade from the spectators. "Uh, I'll see you back at the lodge," he said. "Uh, I might be late." He looked out from under the now thoroughly re-shaped brim of my cowboy hat with a shy little smile. I knew the Stetson was Wes's now.

"So," I said, "I guess the hat worked."

"Thanks," Wes said. He started back toward the parking area where I saw a white van, its engine running, waiting by the exit.

After the last race was run, and the final prize awarded, I started walking back to Nelly Belle, my pickup truck. I pulled the do-rag off my nearly shaved head and wiped the sweat and dust from my face and neck.

"Hey Slim," someone called from behind me. "What happened to your hair?"

I turned and saw a shirtless guy with a single black braid down his brown back. He was half running to catch up with me.

"Hey, how you doing?" He looked familiar but I couldn't place him.

"How about a ride?" he said.

"Where you headed?"

"Wherever you want," he said.

We reached the pickup. "Hop in," I said.

I might have lost my Wyoming Stetson, but I gained a whole camera full of cowboys, and the hottest Indian I'd ever seen was sitting next to me in my truck.

Life at the River, I soon found, revolved around lots of booze, pot, a little cocaine, and a gay roadhouse on River Road called the Rusty Nail. Owned by three lesbians, it was the social center of the gay community. The sheriff's deputies kept a close eye on it. They didn't want to bust the place. The deputies wanted somewhere to take their girlfriends when they were stepping out on their wives. It seemed a win-win situation for everybody. Life at the Rusty Nail revolved around booze, disco dancing, pickups, and more booze.

There was a special drink at the bars the winter I spent at the River. It was called a teeny-tiny. A teeny-tiny was half a shot of Stolichnaya vodka topped off with peppermint schnapps. People would buy themselves a teeny-tiny. They would buy others a teeny-tiny. They would buy the whole bar a teeny-tiny. People would play "liars dice" at the bar for a teeny-tiny. Allan Lowery once came up from the City for a visit. At the Rusty Nail a hot man squeezed in next to Allan at the crowded horseshoe bar.

"Wanna play 'liars dice,' bud?"

"Liars dice?" Allan said. "I don't even know how to play honest men's dice, but I'll go home with you if you're into bondage." They left together.

I ran into Allan another time at the Rusty Nail. He was up at the River with a friend from the City. They were sitting at the bar when I walked in late one Saturday night.

"Jim," Allan called out. He motioned for me to join them. Allan was in full leathers. So was I. The place was packed. "Jim, this is Karl," Allen said. "Karl, Jim."

I shook hands with Karl. He had a firm grip. He wore a pair of faded Levi's and a snug white T-shirt that showed off his trim body. Dark hair with a little gray peeked out of the top of the T-shirt. His short hair also displayed a little gray at the temples. Early 50s, I thought. Buff early 50s.

"What'll you have?" Allen asked me. "Karl's buying." I looked at Karl. A rascal's grin danced about his lips. The bartender grinned at me, waiting.

"Gin and tonic with a squeeze," I said.

"Another vodka martini?" the bartender said to Allan. Allan nodded.

"And another draft for you?" Karl shook his head and looked at his beer. It'd barely been touched.

After a couple more drinks it was last call. Karl was headed for the pisser. "Want to join us?" Allan said. "We're staying at Karl's cottage over by Salmon Creek."

"Sure," I said. "He's hot." Allan and I had worked in tandem with each other before. It was almost a routine. The bar lights came on. The music stopped. We headed for the door. "I'll have to hitch a ride with you guys," I said. "I totaled the truck about a month ago." Allan knew that I said it for Karl's sake.

"You'll fit in the back," Allan said. We were headed for the far edge of the parking lot where some late blooming acacia bushes still scented the night air. There was only one car parked there; a black BMW E21. Last year's model.

I folded myself into the back. We left the parking lot spraying a modest amount of loose gravel, turned left on River Road, and headed for the Pacific.

Salmon Creek is a wide spot in the road on old U.S. 1, just north of Bodega Bay. Karl pulled up and parked in front of his place. The front door was practically on the old road, the lot was so narrow. When we got out, you could hear the late-night groan of the ocean as it hit the beach behind the cottage, some 50 feet below. The cottage had two loft bedrooms tucked under a cathedral ceiling. The rest was open space, with floor-to-ceiling windows and sliding doors onto a deck facing the Pacific. All was finished with bleached wood that looked like it had washed up on the beach below.

I stepped onto the deck, to inhale the smell of the ocean and clear my head a little. I wasn't used to so many gin and tonics. I spotted a length of clothes line tied across the deck. It had a jockstrap attached to it with a couple of wooden snap clothespins. I removed it and put it and the clothespins in my pocket. I untied the clothes line, coiled it, and stuffed it in my hip pocket. I stepped back into the room. Allan had Karl naked, down on the floor, licking his boots. I joined them by putting my own boot next to Allan's.

Before the night was over we had our way with Karl, or he had his way with us. First I tied Karl up with the clothes line in Japanese body bondage. It was a skill Jack Fritscher had taught me years before after a trip to Tokyo. Then Allan tied Karl down to the four poster bed in the loft. Next we took turns disciplining him. I stuffed the jock in Karl's mouth, put the clothespins on his nipples. I alternated my hands, my belt, and a gull feather bouquet from the coffee table, in a drumming tattoo on his back and ass. By sunup we were all blissfully exhausted.

After a nap of a few hours, we were up and revived by some lines of coke that magically appeared. We were out of vodka. I was picked to drive into Bodega Bay on a vodka run. I had only the full leathers I'd worn the night before. The upside? I got to drive the BMW to the convenience store a couple of miles away. I'm not sure which was more titillating for the family daddies picking up the Sunday *Chronicle*. Was it me in full leathers, or the BMW?

Back at the cottage, Karl proved the perfect host. He started with bull shots: vodka and beef bouillon duded up with Tabasco, Worcestershire, lemon and pepper. The perfect way to cleanse Saturday night mouth. An eggs Benedict brunch was followed by feeding the gulls on the deck. Next was a long walk on the beach where we spotted driftwood, sea-glass, and the feathered remains of a brown pelican. After an afternoon nap, Karl again demonstrated his culinary skills by preparing, from scratch, chicken Kiev and a Caesar salad, complete with a raw egg. I filed Karl's cooking skills away for future use.

I was dropped off at my place up Canyon Three Road, in Rio Nido. Allan and Karl returned to the City.

One night, this hot babe walked into the Rusty Nail. She chalked her name on the wall by the pool table and waited her turn. Most of the women in the bar were better pool players than the men. When this babe's turn came up, she beat the pants off dyke after dyke at the pool table. Finally a young sinewy man in a slouched cowboy hat who'd been leaning against the wall waiting his turn, stepped up to the pool table. He beat the pants off the babe.

"I want ya to know," he said when the game ended, "that I'm the token straight guy around here."

"Well, honey, I want you to know," she said, "that I'm the token transsexual. Let's go to your place and token fuck."

They did. I saw her a year later at the Balcony Bar on Market Street in the City. She had a hot hung Hispanic man on her arm. Said they were married. I complimented her on her pool games at the Rusty Nail. She learned to play pool where she grew up in Texas, she said, to keep from getting beat up by the straight bullies.

Thursday night at the River was penny-ante poker and potluck night at Pat Conway's house. Pat was the major owner of the Rusty Nail. She had a house at the back of the canyon, behind her bar, that was California modern, looked out over the tree tops, and took 78 steps to reach the front door.

A larger-than-life marble statue of Hercules, draped in a lion skin, that she'd had shipped from her father's estate in New Jersey, guarded the steps. Her hot tub seated 12 naked people at a time. She had a regulation slate pool table in her living room. It was here that I learned to play poker, improved my pool game, and exchanged potluck recipes.

The job at the Russian River Lodge ended for the season. I moved into a cabin up a canyon near the village of Rio Nido. One rainy night I was following Torch, a Janice Joplin wannabe baby dyke, in her VW bug to an isolated cabin to take publicity pix of a budding River rock group.

As we started up a private mountain road, with no guardrails, I saw a large limb in the road that the storm had taken down. The VW easily went around it. I followed, thinking the road was wide enough for my pickup truck. It wasn't. If I hadn't been playing liars-dice for a teeny-tiny or two I would have seen that. But I had and I didn't.

My truck slid off the road, flipped over, and landed 50 feet down the embankment with the horn blowing. Old Nelly Belle was totaled. I walked away with my camera and a cracked sternum.

I was left without wheels. That meant hitchhiking.

I got a job in the kitchen of the River Village, a cozy gay resort that wanted to extend the season into winter's rainy weather time. River Village was in Rio Nido, within walking distance of my canyon cabin.

I started out as a dishwasher, graduated to salad man, general food prep, learned how to shuck oysters, and within a couple of months I was sous chef. The kitchen tried to follow the mantra of Alice Waters' *Chez Panisse* restaurant in Berkeley, with seasonal and local ingredients. Sometimes they made it, sometimes they didn't. The "Catch of the Day" on the menu really had been pulled from the Pacific hours earlier by two handsome fishermen the manager knew. The job sparked my lifelong interest for local and seasonal cooking.

Michael Palmer, another refugee from the City, moved in with me for a while. One night we decided to hitchhike to the Rusty Nail, about seven miles down River Road. Just off the shoulder of the road, at the bottom of a deep gorge, is the Russian River. The shoulder, where we stood in the dark with our thumbs extended for a ride, was only a few feet wide. I saw a carload of young rednecks, hooting and hollering, headed the opposite direction. They slowed down, then turned around by the postal substation. They started back toward us.

"Michael," I yelled. "Get back here by the edge of the bank."

"Why, what are you talking about?" He hadn't seen the car turn around.

"If we stand here and they try to run us down, we can jump out of the way and they'll plunge their car over the bank and into the river." He still didn't get it until the car was almost back on River Road.

The car came roaring back down the road from Canyon Three Road. It stopped in the middle of the road when they saw where we were standing. It was right under the lone overhead street light at the intersection. I could almost make out their license plate number.

"Get out of Dodge, faggots," somebody yelled out the window.

To their surprise, as well as my own, I started toward the rear of their car. Now I could make out the license plate number.

"079-RNB! 079-RNB! 079-RNB!" I kept yelling their license plate number as loud as I could. There were a few cabins nearby. At least one of them had lights on. Would anybody hear me? The redneck boys finally figured out what I was doing and squealed off toward Guerneville.

"Michael, we have to remember that number!" We both kept repeating it out loud while cars going in our direction whizzed past us. "079-RNB, 079-RNB." Would anybody stop? Finally a pair of headlights slowed down as they approached us. Were the redneck boys back? The lights were so bright we couldn't tell what kind of car it was. It stopped just before it reached us. Then I saw a Mercedes hood ornament. I heard the soft sound of a window being lowered.

"Would you boys like a ride?" a culture-aged voice asked. Would we? You bet your sweet ass we would!

We climbed into the back seat as two perfectly coiffed and immaculately dressed gentlemen turned their smiling faces toward us. They looked in their 80s. Thank-god for rich old ladies of any gender. When we reached the Rusty Nail we invited them to join us for a teeny-tiny. After just a hint of hesitation, they declined.

We called the sheriff's department in Guerneville with the 079-RNB number. We learned later the deputies had stopped the car and talked to its occupants. Since they had not actually done anything to us, except call us faggots, they couldn't arrest them. The boys were warned that if anything happened later, they would be on the top of the sheriff's shit list.

Not quite half way between Guerneville and Jenner by the sea is the little town of Monte Rio. Under the redwoods nearby, on nearly 3,000 acres, is Bohemian Grove. Bohemian Grove is the summer encampment of the Bohemian Club, an all-male fraternity of the most wealthy and powerful men in the country. Founded in San Francisco in the 1870s, the club started accumulating redwood acres in the late 1800s. The Grove, especially during the July encampment , is an all-male fantasy land, where the rich and famous can revert to the adolescent hijinks of a boys summer camp.

As private jets landed at Santa Rosa airport, disgorging the masters of power and wealth, another group of bohemians was quietly converging at the River. They too, came from San Francisco, Los Angeles, and even as far away as Nevada. These modern-day courtesans were part of the fantasy. They knew where the money was.

One night Michael and I decided to hike into Guerneville and out to the Highlands. The Highlands Resort, near the redwoods of Armstrong Woods State Reserve, was a collection of old 1940s-style tourist cabins that had "gone gay." There was a community room with a bar and dance floor, where guests and locals could mingle. We got there early. It was quiet. We both sorted through our pockets for loose change and ordered draft beers.

A young woman in a summer dress came in. As she approached the nearly empty bar, I could tell by the way she walked that she liked being the center of attention. Out of all the empty stools at the bar, she sat on the one next to me. She was so close I could feel the heat from her body. I tried to ignore her by horning in on the conversation Michael was having with the bartender. Michael gave me a dirty look. He was trying to set up something with the bartender for later.

"Well, are you going to buy me a drink or not?" she said.

I turned in her direction and covertly eyed her breasts. They were way out of proportion for her petite body. "I don't have any money," I said. Mammary augmentation implants, I thought.

"Well," she said, "why don't I buy you and your boyfriend a drink then?"

"Sure, why not?" I said. At least she seemed to know the score.

"Bartender," she said. "Get these two gentlemen whatever they want and a margarita for me."

The bartender pulled two draft beers and set them in front of Michael and me. He proceeded to build her margarita.

"When you're done, set up a round of teeny-tinies for us. One for yourself, too," she said.

"You got it," the bartender said. "I'll take mine when I get off."

She reached between her robust breasts and pulled out a rolled-up bill. She unrolled it on the bar. It was a 100-dollar bill. I thought I could see white powder along one edge.

"Can you break that for me?" she said.

"Can do," the bartender said.

For as early and as quiet as it was in the bar, I was surprised. He totaled up all the drinks, including his own teeny-tiny for later, and counted out her change on the bar.

"This is for you, honey," she said. She pushed the coins and a 10-dollar bill toward the bartender. She folded the remaining bills and put them somewhere in her skirt.

"Cheers!" we all said as we downed our Stolichnaya and schnapps.

"Want to dance?" she said, as she stood up, grabbed my hand, and started pulling me toward the dance floor. The sexual energy of the disco music seemed misplaced. Nobody was dancing.

"Want to see something pretty?" she said, when we reached the dance floor. Before I could answer, she unzipped the top of her dress. I realized it wasn't a dress at all but a bustier with a matching wraparound skirt. "Aren't they pretty?" she said. Her mammary augmentation implants were now on full display under the mirrored ball above the empty dance floor. Donna Summers sang on: "Love to Love You Baby." I wasn't sure what to say. She bent over slightly as she danced. Her tits swayed to the rhythm of the music. Then I got it.

"Why'd you come here tonight?" I said.

"Practice," she said.

"Practice?"

"I have an appointment out at Bohemian Grove later tonight," she said. "I always come up here in July when the big boys are at midsummer encampment." She carefully zipped the bustier up around her tits. I felt a little more comfortable.

"But why a gay bar?" I said.

"I'm safe here," she said. "I can try out my act without being hit on."

"And you get yourself turned on for later, out at the Grove?" I said.

"Something like that," she said. "Got to go."

I was just getting interested, not sexually, but in her modus operandi. "But what do you do the rest of the time?" I said, as she started toward the door.

"I teach sociology at San Francisco State," she said over her shoulder as she left.

After 18 months at the River I'd learned to mix a bull shot, make hollandaise sauce, shuck oysters, play penny-ante poker and liars dice, and be wary of a teeny-tiny. As Kenny Rogers says, you got to "know when to fold ›em/Know when to walk away…" I bought an ancient Volvo 544 that had faded to dusty Wedgwood blue and fled the River back to the City.

Camille and Sybil

1979: photo by Jim Stewart at 11th and Folsom Streets, "Nelly Belle," Jim Stewart's GMC pickup truck, parked at curb

Mercedes Headed North on 101

Somewhere between Petaluma
and Santa Rosa
I spotted you heading north

Classic station wagon
an estate car with
original roof rack
filled with brown leather trunks
fastened by brass buckled straps

The faded racing-green finish said
you were not restored
but kept in shape

Your driver
well into his 60s
held his liver-spotted hands
firmly at ten and two
while looking straight ahead
he kept you at 55
long before cruise control

Were you purchased decades ago
in a West German postwar deal
complete with factory tour
or at some long-closed foreign
dealership's polished showroom
on North Van Ness

Is your driver an emeritus professor
in ancient arcane languages
taught at Berkeley or
a retired banker from the City
headed for weekend pleasures
at the Russian River

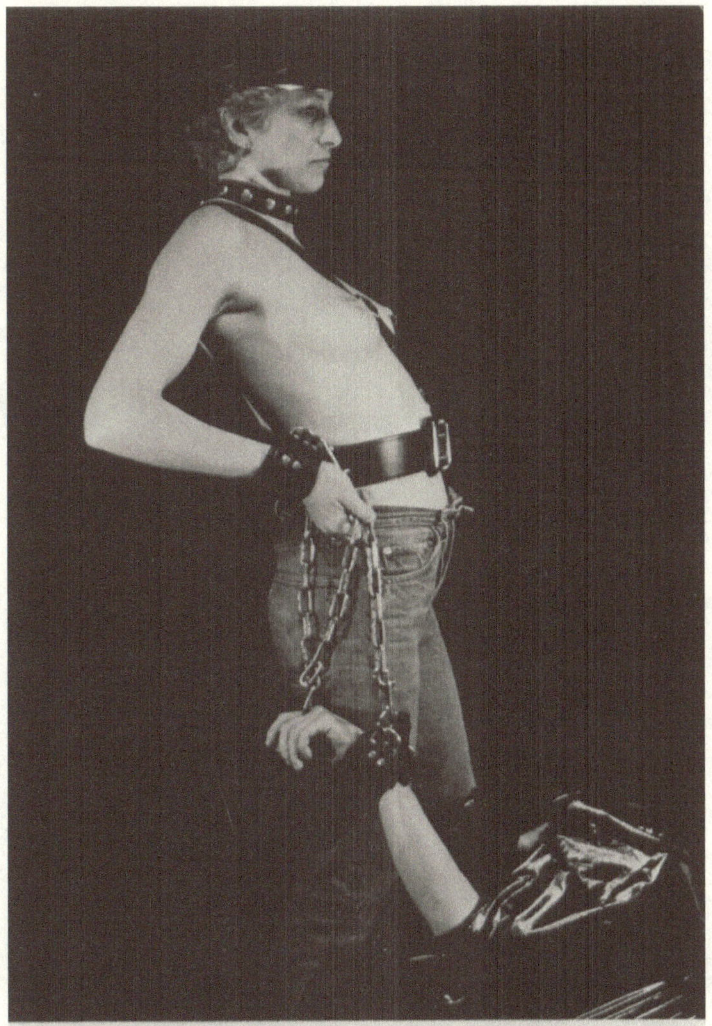

JIM STEWART—PHOTOS
"TOWN AND COUNTRY"
Reception—March 3, 9–11 p.m.
Public—March 4–28, 1982
544 NATOMA, San Francisco, 621-2683

Jim Stewart – Photos: Town and Country

1979: exhibition announcement for 544 Natoma Gallery March, 1982

Lou Rudolph at Keyhole Studios on Clementina Street
1979: photo by Jim Stewart

Steve The Bartender: Drummer Compound

1981: photo by Jim Stewart

Geno The Greek

1982: photo by Jim Stewart

Back from The River

Paul, an early computer geek from Vancouver, British Columbia, worked for Bank of America. He offered his place as a crash pad until I got my feet back on the ground in the City. His apartment, on the seventh floor of a 1920s vintage building on Scott Street, overlooked Alamo Square.

Because of the elevation, his living room windows framed the famous row of Matthew Kavanaugh Painted Ladies lined up on Steiner Street, the other side of the square. With the financial district, the Transamerica Pyramid, and the big black Bank of America building behind them, these are probably the most photographed houses in the City.

Many a man might have offered his left nut to live in a place with this view. Me? I missed the grit of Folsom Street.

I rode the elevator up to the seventh floor one night after returning from a "house call." Dressed in full leathers, I was carrying an old Gladstone bag filled with toys. My "doctor's bag." One toy, a quirt presented to me by a monk, was just a little too long to fit in the Gladstone. It hung enticingly out of the slightly unzipped bag. A mature, but still young, woman shared the elevator as it ascended. After a couple of floors passed in silence, she looked from my doctor's bag to me and back again to the quirt.

"Looks like somebody's going to have a good time tonight."

"Already have."

She smiled knowingly, and got off on the sixth floor.

Allan Lowery's old bar, the Leatherneck, at the corner of 11th and Folsom Streets, was open again. This time around it was owned by John Embry, who also owned *Drummer* magazine. The cesspool in the courtyard had been returned to its pristine beauty as a swimming pool during the place's short interlude as a straight bar.

The bar soon returned to its gay Folsom roots, and was called the Compound. While the bar was open to the public, a private membership allowed after-hours pool use. I heard on the street Embry was looking for a carpenter to built a cage to showcase rough customers. I got the job building the cage. When that was finished, John Embry kept me on as a backup bartender.

It was better than hanging out by Flagg Brothers shoe store with hustlers nearly half my age. Soon I was managing the leather shop in the back. By the end of the second month, photographer/porno star/bar manager JimEd Thompson quit as manager, after a falling out with John Embry. I became de facto manager.

It was a time-consuming job, despite the dismal turnout at the bar. I rarely made it back to Alamo Square at night. Those nights I wasn't invited to somebody's place, or I didn't end up at the baths, I crashed on an army cot in the upstairs office at the bar.

By the end of the month, I officially moved out of Paul's place on Alamo Square and into the office above the bar. It was a tight fit, but I managed to squeeze in an antique walnut commode my great-grandmother had bought in Detroit around the time of Lincoln, plus a few other pieces of furniture not in storage. Taking pride of place was my growing art collection, including a Chuck Arnett, a Tom Hinde, and a Go Mishima.

Ron, a trick from Buffalo, New York, who I brought up to my lair one night after the bar closed, looked around in amazement. His eyes sparkled with cocaine we had shared on the bar downstairs. He looked over my faux military officer's uniform of undeterminable origin, the antique dresser, the art work. In an awed voice he whispered, "Save the Fabergé eggs." For the rest of the night we were a czarist officer and his serf who had fled the Bolsheviks to a garret in Paris. Several times before the sun came up we saved the Fabergé eggs.

Living in the bar proved a continuous high from which there was little downtime. While a dwindling "members only" crowd frolicked poolside late into the night, something else was afoot in the bolted bar. Word soon got out that a private *pas de deux* was often played out there after hours. Once the doors were locked and the lights off, many a fantasy happened in the cage, on the pool table, or over the pinball machine. Afterwards, I would crash on the narrow army cot in the upstairs office. It was still *La Bohème* South of Market in the City of Saint Francis, but time was running out. It was early 1981.

One day Dan Gibson walked into the bar. Dan had worked at the Ambush on Harrison for years. He had been to my Double Exposure show back in 1978, and had been equally impressed with my photos and the flat on Clementina. He'd heard I was "roughing it" at the bar.

"I live in a flat I renovated over on Kissling," Dan said. "I'm looking for a roommate, somebody who can put up with my coke snorting and scotch swilling."

"What's it like?" I said, as I drew us each a beer from the tap. I knew Dan, but not intimately.

"What's it like!" Dan said. "I heard you know all about snorting and swilling."

We both laughed out loud in the empty bar and eyed each other over the top of our beer glasses. This might be interesting. John Embry was getting nervous about my living in the bar. He also didn't like my old Volvo parked outside. Didn't think it lent the right ambience to the bar.

"Come over at noon tomorrow," Dan said, "and I'll show you around." He gave me the address on Kissling.

A few minutes past noon the next day I was knocking on Dan's door. Kissling was an alley street. It dead-ended a couple of houses past Dan's place. Around the corner, at 10th and Howard Streets, the bells of St. Joseph's Church had just finished ringing. Aromas from the handmade burrito shop at the corner wafted up the short street. The place had a foreign feel to it, and only a block and a half from the fever and pitch of Folsom Street.

Dan opened the door.

The flat was a shotgun, laid out like many in the warren of alley streets South of Market. A hallway with rooms on the side led to the kitchen in back. What Dan had done here was magic. Dan was from the South, and had been a professional interior designer. It showed.

His personal space was two rooms at the front: a sitting room with double sliding doors to his bedroom. A fireplace anchored the space with a twist on traditional furnishings. Although wing chairs and a four-poster bed lent elegance to the rooms, a mid-20th century Ames chair and ottoman of molded wood and black leather kept the place from looking prissy.

Dan had done an equally superb mix-and-match job in decorating the rest of the flat. What became my room was in the back, off the kitchen, and close to the bathroom.

What sold me on the deal was the enclosed courtyard off the dining room in the back. It was landscaped as if hidden in the Vieux Carré of New Orleans. The apartment had the only door to this oasis. The only windows besides Dan's that overlooked the courtyard were those of the gay neighbor above Dan's flat and a bank of windows in an empty loft above the burrito shop. The other two sides were windowless brick walls three stories high covered with flowering vines.

"Well, what do you think?" Dan said, as we sat down at the kitchen table. He laid out four lines of blow on a mirror and got out the bottle of scotch. The place was perfect, Dan was a great guy, but still I hesitated. The place seemed more like a "home" than a "flat." I was not interested in a relationship. Not now. Dan must have picked up on my hesitation. He started to laugh.

"No strings attached," he said. "I have my space and entertain in the front. You have your space and entertain in the back. The rest we share. Everything is strictly platonic."

"A done deal," I said. We proceeded to snort the coke and sip the scotch to seal the deal.

The Compound needed something to revive it. It needed a hook to bring people in. John Embry made an arrangement with Chuck Renslow, the owner of the Gold Coast leather bar in Chicago, to rename the bar on the corner of 11th and Folsom the Gold Coast West. This was early 1981. I went to John with some further suggestions.

"What's needed here," I said, "is something to really draw men into this bar. A name change alone won't do it."

"Well, do you have something in mind?"

I did. "What musical is really drawing in the crowds right now?"

"*Annie*?"

"Try *Sweeney Todd*." The Demon Barber of Fleet Street, after conquering London's West End and New York, was on the road, and had just opened in San Francisco. People were flocking to it. "Remember 'Inside Sweeney Todd's,' the spread you did in *Drummer* a couple of years ago, on the specialty barbershop on Christopher Street in New York? Well, what about opening our own Sweeney Todd's barbershop right here in the bar?"

"Do you know a barber we can get?"

"As a matter of fact I do." Ron, the Fabergé egg man from Buffalo, was a trained barber and beautician. He was looking for work. He had managed to stay in the City by winning go-go boy contests and scouting out free buffet spreads the bars offered to draw in hot young men. I was sure he would work for a small salary plus the big tips he could pull in. It was a go.

We closed the bar for a week. When it reopened, one former storage room featured a used barber chair, with a restraint table in another. A screen hung from the ceiling in the main bar room. Patrons could watch live action being filmed from a new sex toy, a video camera suspended over the barber chair. It showed the haircuts and shavings being done in Sweeney Todd's barbershop. A second video camera hung over the restraint table, for similar live "broadcasts."

The reopening night of the Gold Coast West saw lines of men down the sidewalk, waiting to get in. A spread of meat pies, both chicken and beef, depending on your taste, was offered. It took a while for many to realize they could watch a BDSM scene or a body shaving on the screen and then walk a few feet and see it live. The bar was off to a great new start. I gave it six months.

About 2:30 one morning in July, after work, I was walking home to Kissling Street. I heard several sirens racing down Folsom. They sounded as if they were headed east. I looked in that direction. The sky was lit with flames. I ran back to Folsom Street. An army of men, mostly fresh from the recently closed bars, had gathered and was headed east. I joined them.

"What's burning?" I said, to the man in the leather chaps and open vest next to me. He wore no shirt. I think I had served him a couple of beers in the bar before he had headed back to the Sweeney Todd barbershop over an hour ago. He still wore a mat of dark curly hair on his chest and displayed a steel gray jarhead hair cut. I had a good idea what had been shaved.

"Looks like it's the old Barracks building," he said, as we passed 9th Street. The crowd grew bigger as we hurried east along Folsom. "When did the Barracks shut down?"

"A few years ago," I said. "It must have been sometime in 1976, because it was after all the Bicentennial celebrations."

The old Folsom Street Barracks bathhouse had been on the south side of the street between 7th and 8th. There it stood now, the four-story blazing remains of what had once been an enticing labyrinth welcoming both Theseus and Minotaur to the mysteries of fantasy sex.

Now fire trucks, their sirens silent while their red lights continued blinking, blocked Folsom Street. Young firemen dragged hoses as close as possible to the flaming structure, shooting water into the inferno. Buildings next door were watered down to contain the blaze. Men holding hoses were hoisted high into the night sky on ladders to spray down into the blaze.

"Do you remember your first time in the Barracks?" the hirsute leatherman next to me said.

"I was here on Bastille Day 1975, for vacation. I had never been in an orgy room before. The minute I was dragged into the room the aroma of male musk overcame me. I was intoxicated. I went wild. I…" I turned back to the leatherman. He was gone. With a great roar the roof of the old Barracks collapsed into the building, sending a display of fireworks high into the night sky. I turned back toward the street.

News vans were parked near the intersection of 8th and Folsom. I walked toward them, stepping around puddles and over leaky fire hoses. There, in the flashing lights, former supervisor—now mayor—Dianne Feinstein was being interviewed.

I walked back toward 7th Street. The flames from the rapidly disintegrating bathhouse painted surrounding buildings with the flickering flames of hell, born in the mind of Hieronymus Bosch. Fantasy sex scenes from long ago were released and flew with the flames into the night sky.

I went into the Stables, a leather bar on Folsom, past the burning Barracks. Joe, a redheaded friend of mine from Michigan, was behind the bar. He had lost weight since moving to the City. His forearms were no longer decorated with heavy coin-silver and turquoise bracelets, gifts from a former sugar daddy. His bloodshot eyes and the slight tremor in his hands when he poured my scotch suggested he might have pawned them for drugs. He was working shirtless in a leather harness. His hippie long red hair was now a crew cut. He looked hot. How long will he last, I wondered.

"Double scotch on the rocks?" he said.

"Sure," I said. How long will I last, I wondered.

Less than a month after a meager celebration of the 1982 New Year, the bar closed. I'd been right. I'd given it six months after the grand reopening the previous July. I was out of a job. Again.

I sat at the bar in Fe-Be's, the old man's leather hangout. I was sipping my second scotch on the rocks when a familiar-looking leatherman straddled the stool next to mine.

"Jim Stewart," he said. "I'd heard you were back from the River."

"Lou Rudolph!" The name came to me in the nick of time. "It's been ages."

I hadn't seen Lou Rudolph—leatherman, painter, performance artist extraordinaire—for nearly three years. I'd shot a special promo photo session with Lou and Sybil, also a performance artist and actor, at my place in early 1979. Lou had been impressed with how I had captured Camille. He wanted to see if I could capture him as well. The shoot went great. We were all pleased with the results.

"Yes, I was at the River. For 18 months. I came back a year ago this month."

"Any photo shows lately?" Lou said.

I drained the last of the scotch from the ice in my glass. "Well, no," I said.

"Get us a couple more," Lou said to the bartender. We were the only customers in the place. "Here," Lou said in a low voice when the bartender left to get our drinks. I felt him place something in my hand.

Instinctively I knew what it was. I turned away from the bar, and pushed it up first one side of my nose and then the other. "Ahhh. Thanks," I said, and put it back in his hand just as the bartender arrived with our drinks.

"Are we ready to talk?" Lou said with a grin.

"We're ready to talk," I said. I snorted my nose and lit up another Marlboro.

"Ever hear of 544 Natoma Performance Gallery?"

"No. That must be down a ways on Natoma."

"Between 6th and 7th. It's a performance gallery that Peter Hartman set up."

I wasn't sure who Peter Hartman was. Lou signaled the bartender for another round. I shook my head no, but it was too late. I felt the little plastic coke bullet in my hand again. What the hell.

"Sounds interesting. Where do I fit in?" My performance pieces had always been one-on-one in The Other Room on Clementina. That was all gone now. My lease had expired while I was at the River. Taylor of San Francisco had moved his leather business and personal performances up one floor into my old flat.

"I'm their 'artist in residence,'" Lou said. "I do nightly performance pieces. We usually hang some artist's work there for a month. It's not much, but it does provide exposure."

"I see…"

"I showed Peter some of the work you had done of Sybil and me. He was impressed. Are you interested in hanging a show there?"

"I might be." Boy, might I ever, I thought. This was just the sort of thing I had hoped might come along. "What's the setup?"

We discussed percentages, printing, framing, and setup costs. We came to a mutually agreeable arrangement, shook hands and Lou left. My hands were shaking as I drained the last of my scotch from the glass.

Would I be able to pull it off? I no longer had my darkroom. My last photos were of anonymous cowboys at the Russian River rodeo outside Guerneville. I did have some shots I had done of Luc and Linda, a dyke I met at the Balcony Bar a few years ago. The pix of Lou and Sybil had never been hung, as well as a few other odds and ends that had never been on public display.

Of course, I could pull it together. This was only the middle of February and the show wasn't due to open until the 3rd of March! I walked home and pulled out my big brown leather suitcase, home to my negatives and contact prints.

I realized later I should have given more thought to the title of my show. Since it would include photos expressing both urban grit and rural guts I called the show "Town and Country." Wrong. The very words suggest a night at the opera followed by a morning fox hunt.

The 544 Natoma Performance Gallery was a cutting-edge space that showcased the emerging urban trash punk scene. I picked the right lead photo for the fliers and posters. It was a high contrast black and white tableau of a dominatrix pulling a chained, bound, male arm from a black plastic trash bag. "Trash" would have been a better title for the show. I should have talked with Lou a little more about his performance piece, "Cheap Hotel." We could have merged the two concepts to present a raw, gritty, urban environment.

I also should have examined the hanging space before choosing the photos. The space was not a formal gallery. Viewers could not get close to most of the photos to examine them. Fewer, but larger, photos would have stood out better.

Lastly, since I no longer had my darkroom, I had to have the prints done by a professional studio. The printer on Folsom Street I had used for the large blowup of Camille was out of business. I chose a place on 18th Street near Castro. While they could print perfectly acceptable prints of your vacation, no matter how graphic they might be, they could not deliver the quality of print I needed for a show. Even matted and framed, the difference was obvious.

Maybe some miracle would pull off the show. There had recently been the case of a show in a gallery on Market Street where buckets of red paint had been splashed on the paintings because some group or another had deemed the works politically incorrect. The news hit the art world. Out of the debacle the artist got a show in New York. My hopes rose when one of the post card reception invitations was returned in an envelope. The bare breasts of the dominatrix photo had big red Xs drawn on them. On the back in angry red letters I was castigated for bringing such "Trash" to a Filipino family neighborhood. I sensed the writer was not Filipino, but rather another advocate of political correctness. I really should have titled the show "Trash." Alas, there were no buckets of red paint. No show in New York.

The night of the opening reception, 544 Natoma was packed. Lou wrote "Cheap Hotel" backwards from behind a sheet strung across the stage. Some feat! His stage performance paintings were greeted with great applause. So were the drag queen performances and Kabuki theater pieces.

By the end of the month I hadn't sold enough works to cover my expenses. I wasn't sure what to do with the stack of matted and framed photos.

Henry, an All-American Boy from Wisconsin, came into Fe-Be's one afternoon as I sat nursing a scotch on the rocks.

"Have you seen this?" he said, as he held out a copy of the *Bay Area Reporter*. He was shaking the weekly bar rag so much for emphasis that nobody could possibly have read what he was pointing to. "It's lifted from a New York gay rag. It says right here, 'Gay pneumonia' is hitting the New York community. Have you heard of this? Gay pneumonia?" He looked first at the bartender who had come up to take his order, then at me, then back again. The bartender shook his head and raised his eyebrows at Henry.

"Draft," Henry said to the bartender.

"Gay pneumonia? How could there be such a thing? Pneumonia can't know if you're gay or not," I said.

"It says right here, 'gay pneumonia,'" Henry said as he stabbed his thick forefinger at the weekly issue of *B.A.R.*

"There was an article last week on 'gay cancer.' I thought the same thing," the bartender said, as he set down Henry's beer. "How can cancer know if you're gay or not?" He glanced at me. "Another?" he said, as he looked at my empty glass. I nodded.

"Let me see that," I said to Henry. "Where are they getting this from anyway?"

The bartender set down my fresh scotch on the rocks and returned to washing glasses.

I sat sipping scotch at the kitchen table in the back of the flat one afternoon, wondering what direction to steer my life. I was 39 and out of a job. There was a loud pounding on the door. I crept to the front and peeked out the drapes. It was Jim Moss.

"Come in, come in," I said. How you been?"

"Busy," Moss said. Jim Moss was a fantasy photographer whose work had been published in *Drummer*.

"I bet," I said. "I've seen a couple of issues of your new magazine, *Folsom*. Hot."

"Thanks," he said. "That's what I came over to talk about."

I hope it's not photos, I thought. After the disappointment of my show at 544 Natoma I wanted to lay low in that department for awhile. I had nothing new to offer.

"I want to show you something," Moss said. We headed for the kitchen table. "Slide that over here," Moss said as we sat down at the table.

I slid my beveled antique coke mirror with the single-edged razor blade on it across the table in front of Moss. He opened a bindle and scraped a quarter of the white powder onto the mirror with the razor blade. He carefully refolded the bindle and laid it on the table. He proceeded to divide the blow into four equal lines.

"You first," he said. I picked up a silver straw by the side of the mirror and snorted two of the lines.

"Ahhh. Great," I said. I handed Moss the silver straw. He snorted the two remaining lines. We both lit a cigarette.

"Scotch?" I said.

"No. No alcohol. I've quit drinking," Moss said. "It was getting out of control."

I glanced at the melted ice and pale scotch in my glass on the table. I left it there.

"Now, what I wanted to show you," he said, as he opened the manila envelope he had brought with him. He pulled out three fine-point ink drawings and laid them on the table. They were various angles of a leather-clad motorcycle rider. One was reflected in the mirror of the motorcycle. I had once done a photo of Ron Clute like that, under the Leatherneck sign, as a promo piece for Allan Lowery's bar.

"Hot," I said. I looked at the signature. It rang no bells. I wasn't sure where I fit into all this.

"What I need," Moss said, "is someone to write a story to go with these drawings. I want it as hot and crisp as the drawings. No more than six pages, double spaced." He drew on his cigarette and slowly French-inhaled. "Can you do that?"

I eyed the watery scotch and French-inhaled my Marlboro. "Yes."

"I'll pay you $100. If I like it. You'll be published in the next issue of my *Folsom* magazine."

"And if you don't like it?"

"You'll be out your time but free to publish it, without the drawings, wherever you want."

"Deal," I said. We both stood up and shook hands.

"Oh, keep that to get you started," Moss said. He nodded at the generous remains in the bindle on the table. "No charge." He left.

I dumped the watery scotch in the sink, put two fresh ice cubes in my glass, and filled it with Cutty Sark.

Two days later I'd snorted the rest of the bindle, emptied the bottle of scotch, burned through three packs of Marlboros, and had a six-page story about a young biker's initiation into fist-fucking in a hunting cabin in Michigan. I walked the story over to Jim Moss's place on Folsom Street.

Jim Moss had a bright green parrot at his place. As soon as I came in the bird flew freely about the room several times before returning nervously to its cage. Piles of parrot shit decorated the newly refinished hardwood floor. I sat on a lone high metal stool, hoping the bird liked me. Moss sat reading my fisting tale at his metal army desk, the only other piece of furniture in the all-white room. He finished and stood up.

"Well, to tell you the truth," Moss said.

Here it comes, I thought, the verbal rejection slip.

"It's the best damn piece of writing anyone's ever submitted to me," Moss said. He laid the manuscript on his desk and unlocked one of its drawers. He handed me a 100-dollar bill. It was curled slightly and I detected a white residue along one edge. The parrot emerged from its cage, then flew around the room a couple of times before leaving its deposit near the cage.

"Can I make a copy?" I said, nodding at the copier on the desk.

"Sure."

By the time I finished copying my fisting story Moss had four lines laid out on a mirrored tile on the desk. We completed the usual ritual. I headed for Fe-Be's.

Henry was at Fe-Be's. By the time I sat down at the bar there was a scotch on the rocks waiting for me.

"Remember that article on 'gay cancer' that was in the B.A.R. last week?" Henry said.

"Who could forget?" the bartender said. He lit my cigarette. I tipped well.

"Well, there's more to it than we thought," Henry said. He lit his own cigarette. I sipped my scotch. "The mainline press has picked up on it," he said. "'Gay' pneumonia turns out to be something called Pneumocystis pneumonia and 'gay' cancer is something called Kaposi's sarcoma."

"Cancer and pneumonia can't know somebody's gay," I said.

"Well, health officials seem to think so. They're lumping the two together and calling it GRID."

"GRID," I said. "What's that mean?"

"Gay-Related Immune Deficiency."

Henry signaled for another round of drinks. The bartender obliged.

"What's this?" Henry said, picking up the manila envelope with the copy of my story inside.

"It's a dirty story I wrote."

"Oh, a dirty story. I love dirty stories. Can I read it?"

"Maybe. What's it worth to you?"

I felt a little plastic coke dispenser being slipped into my hand. "Just don't lose it," I said. "It's the only copy I have."

About a week later, Jim Moss dropped by the house to show me the printer's galley proof for my story. The print was curved to follow the shape of the ink drawings of the biker. It looked very professional. It looked hot! It was my first story in print. Well, almost in print.

We shared a couple of lines at the kitchen table in celebration. Moss spotted the Cutty Sark bottle on the counter. He said he had to leave. He was still on the wagon. I headed for Fe-Be's. Henry was at the bar.

"You look pretty glum," I said. "What happened?"

"My roommate found a couple of spots on his chest this morning."

"You don't mean…"

"They're not sure. They did some tests. We should know by next week sometime."

"Henry, I'm so sorry…" I didn't know what more to say. I bought him a drink. This time it was my turn to slip a little plastic dispenser into Henry's hand.

"Something else. You're going to hate me," he said.

"What?"

"I left your story on the bus. I'm sorry, but there was so much on my mind."

"Don't worry. It's going to be published soon. Then there'll be copies everywhere."

A week later I ran into Jim Moss. He looked pretty glum too. "All right," I said. "What happened? You fall off the wagon?"

"I'm broke. I don't even have the rent."

"What about *Folsom* magazine?" I said.

"Dead. I have no money to put out the next copy. The last issue was the last issue." The afternoon wind came down Folsom Street with fog and a chill. "Don't worry," Moss said. "I'm not asking for the hundred bucks back I paid you for your story."

I snorted a laugh at the idea he would ask such a thing. I nudged Moss into the sheltered doorway of an empty building there on Folsom Street and pressed my plastic coke dispenser into his hand.

"Thanks," he said.

I'd been out of work since January. My finances were in shambles. I'd turn 40 in less than six months. My last photo show had been a flop. My first short story to be published was not going to be published after all. I lit up a cigarette, laid out two lines on my mirror, and freshened my glass with Cutty Sark. By the time the drink was finished and the coke was gone, I'd made up my mind.

In the past I'd always sought solace in academe during times of personal change. Both when my marriage was disintegrating and when I was coming out to myself as a gay man, I had headed for campus. Grad school provided structure with a certain bohemian zest.

By 1982, my life had shifted. My 18 months at the River was a line of demarcation. Although they were hard to pinpoint, there were subtle changes in my post-River life South of Market. Like Hemingway's Paris of the 1920s, my existential San Francisco had been a specific place, during a specific time, and populated with specific people. Then things changed. The very zeitgeist of that life changed.

I was on the cusp of being a newly minted 40-year-old man. A man I wasn't sure of yet, but one who was suddenly concerned with job benefits, heath insurance, and a retirement pension.

After much letter writing, phone queries, and filling out of forms, it was settled. I would return to Western Michigan University for a second master's degree. This one in library science. It was time for a mid-life career change.

Train travel intrigued me. I had ridden many trains in Europe. My rail travel here had been limited to a few trips between Kalamazoo and Chicago. Now I wanted to experience a cross country train trip. I packed up what was left of my goods and shipped them via motor freight to Michigan. Two suitcases I'd take on the train. The smaller one held a few clothes and a toothbrush. The larger rather ratty brown leather suitcase held my camera, photo negatives, and contact sheets. I was taking no chances it would be lost en route.

How do you say goodbye to San Francisco? You never can. I wanted to leave town quietly, promising myself I'd return. My last night in the City I spent at the Caldron, a piss palace a couple of blocks away on Natoma. In the morning Wil Rutland, a lanky North Carolinian I'd run into several times at the Caldron, drove me in his 1959 red Cadillac convertible to the Transbay Terminal at Mission and First. The sun was out. The top was down. I boarded a bus that took me over the Oakland Bay Bridge to the Amtrak station and a train bound for Chicago.

Sweetbreads

Ah, Sweetbreads, what night will I see you again?
Will you deliver your warm earthy flavors to me
In the rustic urban setting of Café Noir's low ceilinged
Hideaway on Upper Market Street where we first met
By chance after sundown on a Thursday in November?

I came late with no reservations
I stole you
I had no choice
It was you or that *Poulet Basquaise*
Many have had you
I know
But for me it was my very first time.

Will I climb the narrow steep stairs on Romolo Place
Some Tuesday to find you being passed around by
Rough young workers' hands down some long
Boardinghouse table as the daily special braised
With Madeira for any displaced West Coast Basque?

Our former meeting place has changed from
Crowded cellar bistro to bistrotheque to a small Korean bar.
I've moved east now and dine on Lake Superior whitefish
While you my dear are Basquing in your new-found glory
As contemporary taste trendsetters
Abduct you for their very own.

766 Clementina Street

2008: photo by Jim Stewart

Epilogue

The westbound California Zephyr No. 5 from Chicago was due into Emeryville at 5:10 p.m. Pacific time. It arrived at 9:08, nearly four hours late. Ken, my partner of 25 years, and I detrained and boarded the Amtrak bus. The bus came off the Oakland Bay Bridge and entered the City. I'd kept the promise I'd made to myself over a quarter of a century before. I'd come back to San Francisco.

As I'd planned, I returned to grad school and earned another master's degree, this one in library science. For the next 20 years I lived in Chicago. I worked for the Chicago Public Library, first as a government documents librarian and then as head of the history department.

I'd done doctoral work at the University of Illinois Chicago, with emphasis on American migrant groups. I'd started work on my dissertation, *The Detroit French in the Early Republic.* But I had retired with an ABD, all but dissertation. After retiring, Ken and I moved to the West Shore of Michigan and a restored mid-19th-century farmhouse that has been in my family since it was built.

Now, back in San Francisco, at night, the City seemed different. From near the renovated Ferry Building, once a rundown hulk left from a pre-bridge era, brightly lit high rise buildings hid the distinctive shape of the Transamerica Pyramid, as much a symbol of San Francisco as the Golden Gate Bridge.

Finally, an empty cab on busy Market Street took us to our reserved boutique hotel on Bush Street near Powell, the cable car street. It was after 11 p.m. We went out for a late supper.

I looked west on Bush Street and saw the brightly lit marquee of the Nob Hill Theatre. It enticed you to visit their video arcade or see an all-male strip show. A few young men were standing around in a knot by the entrance. As we crossed Powell Street, a cable car came clanging up the hill. Standing at the corner was a young hustler. He followed us into the Roxanne Café.

"Three?" the Vietnamese hostess said. She picked up three menus.

I turned around. The hustler was striking up a conversation with Ken. Some things in San Francisco never change.

"No, just two," I said ruefully. It'd already been a very long day.

The Fettuccini Roxanne was delish.

The next day we explored San Francisco, like tourists. We bought Muni Metro passes and rode both the Powell and California Street cable cars. We went to Fishermen's Wharf and had Dungeness crab cakes. We wended our way through the renovated Ferry Building and browsed through overpriced kitchen wares and bought ridiculously delicious chocolates.

The second day in San Francisco was my day of reckoning.

"I'm sure my flat on Clementina is gone," I said. "Most likely replaced by a high-rise condo. I'm not sure if I want to look."

"You'll never know if you don't look," Ken said. "If you don't look, I'll hear about it forever."

We walked south on 9th Street from Market Street. As we crossed Howard Street I saw the Lebanese mom-and-pop grocery store still stood at the corner of Tehama Alley. The liquor sign was more prominent than it had been. I remembered buying a bottle of Courvoisier there with Joelle one Christmas eve after a midnight service at Grace Cathedral. Joelle and her girlfriend had moved down the peninsula, had a baby, and gone MIA.

I glanced in the direction where my flat on Clementina Alley had been. No high-rises reared into the sky. I quickened my pace. Here was the corner. "Clementina End." The street sign was still there. We rounded the corner. There it stood. The shingles I'd nailed up the summer of 1976 were weathered, but still there. The brown trim was faded, but still there. I started to weep.

"You better give me the camera if you want some pictures," Ken said. I gave him the camera.

The place had changed a little. Two gigantic dusty jade plants in weathered pots now stood guard by the steps. A metal security gate protected the doors. The basement window had been filled in with glass bricks.

I thought of my front door I easily kicked open one night when I forgot my keys. I could have knocked since Luc was upstairs. It was easier to kick it in.

I thought of Luc, who had moved to Paris, taken a lover, and got real film roles in French cinema. He had been in a film with Isabelle Adjani, a feat he loved to brag about when he visited me in Chicago in 1989. We had both seen her in Francois Truffaut's *The Story of Adele H.* in San Francisco. Luc died of AIDS the summer of 1991.

My old hangouts South of Market were gone. The Ambush and Fe-Be's had both closed the summer of 1986. Allan Lowery's Leatherneck and the *Drummer* Compound were history before I left the City. The last I had heard Allan was living in Denver. He was now MIA.

A young man opened the security gate, came down the cement steps with a basket of laundry, and entered the basement. What sort of fantasies was he living in my old flat? I didn't want to know. Like unrequited love, sometimes not knowing can be more exciting than knowing and being disappointed.

"Do you want pictures of anything else?" Ken said. I was back in the present.

"Yes," I said. "I want a picture on Howard Street where Robert Opel's Fey-Way Studios used to be." We hiked back up 9th Street to Howard. I squinted, trying to visualize the first homomasculine art gallery in San Francisco.

Yes. There it was, back from the corner a little, 1287 Howard Street. It was no longer the leather art gallery created by Robert Opel, the Academy Awards streaker. Wild opening night invitation-only parties were a thing of the past. It was no longer a crime scene where Robert Opel had been mysteriously murdered and Camille O'Grady and Anthony Rogers threatened. The yellow crime tape was long gone.

The post-earthquake building was now a renovated four-flat at a tony address in SoMa. I wondered if the people living there now were ever visited by the ghosts of the building's past. Less than a year after my San Francisco trip I was visited by such a ghost. Robert Oppel, Robert Opel's nephew who spelled his name with a double "p," was filming *Uncle Bob.* I was filmed in an interview recalling my relationship with Robert Opel over a quarter of a century earlier. Little did I know then, that the ghosts of Fey-Way Studios would visit me yet again. In 2010, photos I had taken of Camille O'Grady with skull, and Robert Opel with skull in 1979, were picked by San Francisco Camerawork, a major SoMa gallery, as part of a retrospective show, "An Autobiography of The San Francisco Bay Area Part Two: The Future Lasts Forever."

The Castro was next on my list. We walked back to Market Street and took a restored green and cream antique trolley up Market to 17th Street and Castro. The first time I lived in San Francisco, the summer of 1965, these cars had been for real. Some of the seats then were still upholstered in real leather, frayed at the corners. Replacement covers were Naugahyde. Riding those trolleys then I learned to recognize real leather, a skill that proved useful. I picked up a black leather tuxedo couch once at an unclaimed freight warehouse South of Market. It was marked and priced Naugahyde.

When Ken and I got off at the end of the line, he spotted the Twin Peaks sign. The same sign had been there close to 30 years.

"Is that the same place we saw in the Milk film?" Ken said.

"The very same," I said. Three times we had watched Sean Penn portray Harvey in *Milk*.

"And the Castro Theatre," Ken said. We'd rounded the corner onto Castro Street and there stood the queen of gay theaters. "Well, what do you want to do?" It was early afternoon.

"Let's just walk around for a while," I said. "Get a feel for the place." We walked down Castro to 18th Street. After we had passed the Castro Theatre, nothing looked familiar. We started up the hill towards 19th Street. Although it was a warm sunny afternoon, as is often the case in San Francisco in September, something was missing. No hordes of shirtless, forever-buff men displayed their well-endowed crotches for admiration. No disco music blasted from the bars. No one tried to sell us dope.

As we neared the intersection of 19th Street, I glanced up Castro Street and spotted the building where Sheldon Kovalski had last lived. I called Sheldon in 1989, after the earthquake. We talked for a long time. He had AIDS. He said he was going to stop taking his meds. I never heard from him again.

"Let's get an ice tea," I said. We were now men of a certain age. We settled ourselves into café chairs on the sidewalk outside a small desert shop on 19th Street.

"No sugar," I heard Ken tell the server. There was one other couple at this small sidewalk café. A middle-aged lesbian was very seriously going over some organizational plans with an extremely handsome young Hispanic man. No, I thought, this can't be the Castro.

Walking back down on the other side of the street, we saw a couple of young Asian men holding hands.

"Let's cross over and go in the bookstore," Ken said. We were nearly up to Market Street. It was close to the Castro Theatre. We crossed over and went in. After 20 years as a librarian, the first thing I did was look for the book organization scheme. I couldn't find one.

"Can you tell me if you have a certain book?" I said. Two guys talking at the counter looked at me slightly annoyed. The one from behind the counter came over. "Do you carry Jack Fritscher's new work, *Gay San Francisco: Eyewitness Drummer*?" I said.

"I don't know," the sales clerk said. He went back to the counter, consulted a computer. "Yes," he said. "We have one copy." He turned back to his friend and resumed their conversation.

"Could you show me where it is?" I said.

Without a word he left the counter, looked in three different places, finally found the book displayed with only its spine showing. He pulled it from the shelf, and without a word, handed it to me. He went back to his friend at the counter.

"Thanks," I said. I thumbed through it, admiring my own photos Jack had been so gracious to use in his magnum opus. I looked up. Ken was waiting on the sidewalk. I laid the book, cover up, on a table prominently labeled "New Books" and walked out.

"Hungry?" I said. We turned the corner and started down 17th Street. I hadn't noticed when we got off the trolley but now I saw it was still there. The big red and white Coca-Cola sign hung out over the sidewalk.

Orphan Andy's opened sometime after I moved to San Francisco in 1975. Alice Waters was just launching the local and seasonal food trend at her Chez Panisse restaurant in Berkeley then. Except for the Norse Cove, Castro Street eateries had been pretty much home cooking and comfort food. Orphan Andy's still is. We each had a Monte Cristo from the 24-hour menu. They were delish.

We decided to take the Muni Metro back. We got on the inbound M Ocean View line at the Castro station in Harvey Milk Square. We got off at Powell Street and waited with our three-day passes for the cable car to return us up the hill to our hotel on Bush Street.

In the morning I picked up the Ford Escape Hybrid I'd reserved at the Budget car rental across the street. We crossed the Golden Gate Bridge. The rainbow above the tunnel was still there.

"Are you nervous?" Ken said.

"A little." I knew what he meant. We were headed north on Highway 101 to Sonoma County.

We were going to visit Jack Fritscher and his spouse, Mark Hemry, who lived in the country outside of Sebastopol. After nearly three decades, Jack Fritscher and I had reconnected via the internet. In August, 2007, I had emailed Jack: "While doing research for a project I came across your *Drummer* review, 'Introducing Jim Stewart.' I'm flattered. Thank you." My project was this book.

Jack emailed back: "You make me so happy, to know you are alive and not lost, and that you are doing well, and partnered, and creating. Thank God." For a year we emailed regularly. Now we were meeting again after 30 years.

After so many years, nothing looked familiar on Highway 101. Then I saw the Marin County Courthouse.

"Look," I said. "Frank Lloyd Wright." Ken swiveled his head

around to see the last building designed by the 20th century's master of American architecture. I had pointed it out as a distraction. We both knew it. We rode on in silence, observing the northern California countryside. We left the highway. Ken went into high gear as co-pilot and map reader. We arrived.

My worries about such a reunion were all for naught. The visit was splendid. We were wined and dined and squired around Sonoma County in Volvo style. On Monday morning, Jack and Mark drove us to Santa Rosa, where they were both our witnesses and our photographer as Ken and I were legally married. This was during that small window of California legal sanity from May 15, 2008, to November 4, 2008, when Proposition 8 was passed, outlawing further same-sex marriages in the state. That's another tale.

We drove back to San Francisco. Lunch at the Beach Chalet on the Great Highway near the end of Golden Gate Park was superb. The WPA frescoes by Lucien Labaudt in the Chalet captured the spirit of 1930s San Francisco as much as the wild mushroom pizza with local goat cheese and truffle oil captured the California Slow Food movement. After lunch we walked along the Pacific and listened to the breakers.

We drove out to Lands End. It was no longer a forbidden enclave of feral cats, abandoned cellars, naked men, and wild sex. The parking lot was paved, the grounds groomed. We sat on a bench and watched an octogenarian being fawned over by her middle-aged sons. All were dressed as if for bit parts in a Bernardo Bertolucci film.

A Chinese freighter, piled high with containers of foreign goods, passed under the Golden Gate Bridge and headed east toward Oakland. Lands End had been tamed.

We dropped off our bags at the small Amtrak station on the Embarcadero, dropped the Ford off at the car rental place on Bush Street, and caught the cable car down Powell. We had a disappointing supper on Geary Street at Max's, the former Pam Pams, where streetwalkers, drag queens, leathermen, and theater folk had all once gathered after the bars closed. The place now displayed a weak attempt at elegance and manufactured atmosphere.

We strolled down Market Street toward the Ferry Building. Where Market meets Bush and Battery Streets, we came upon the Mechanics Monument. This 1899 bronze work by Douglas Tilden of five nearly naked workmen driving a punch through a metal plate stopped us in our tracks. I thought I had photographed this once, only to discover the film had not advanced in my Nikon. Again we were out of film.

At Justin Herman Plaza, by the Ferry Building, we rested in the dusk, and watched shirtless boys casually competing on their skateboards. We saw the 1940s-style F-line yellow-and-gray streetcar with green stripes pass on the Embarcadero. I felt again as if in a foreign country. We walked across the street and boarded the Amtrak bus for Emeryville.

George Cory and Douglass Cross, gay lovers, remind us in their famous song that when we leave, we leave our hearts in San Francisco. But then sometimes we do leave. Sometimes we leave because our lives change. Because places change. Because times change. I had changed. When I left San Francisco in 1982, I was no longer the man who arrived in 1975. I had ripened into middle age, with no regrets. I could see beyond my magnificent obsession with the fever and pitch of the immediate hour. The City itself had changed. The most open and liberal and beautiful city in American had been plagued by assassinations and murder. Discord had come with pestilence and death. In 1982 the very zeitgeist had changed, not just in San Francisco, but across the country, as California's former governor settled into power in Washington. San Francisco had been a place in a time that had given me inner strength as a gay man. By 1982 it was time to test that mettle in a wider world. I left my heart in San Francisco. Decades later I returned. I still loved San Francisco, but knew I was no longer in love with San Francisco. San Francisco was a once-upon-a-time lover. One I remembered fondly, but one whose name I no longer called out passionately in the heat of the night. Better still, San Francisco had become my *Moveable Feast*, one that still nourishes me and that I will carry with me always.

Jim Stewart (b. 1942) grew up on a farm in Michigan. He earned his undergraduate degree in history at Michigan State University, master's degrees in history and librarianship at Western Michigan University, and completed course work toward a Ph.D. in American history at the University of Illinois Chicago. He taught history and English before managing a foreign-and-art-film theater in Kalamazoo, Michigan. He spent the late 1970s in San Francisco where he lived South of Market. There he practiced photography, founded Keyhole Studios, and was much published in *Drummer* magazine. He had five shows and various group shows in the early SoMa galleries of the late 1970s. In 2010, his work was represented at SF Camerawork gallery in "An Autobiography of the San Francisco Bay Area Part 2: The Future Lasts Forever." He returned to the Great Lakes area where he was head of the history department at the Chicago Public Library. He now lives with his partner of over 25 years on Michigan's west shore. He is currently working on a mystery novel.

Jim Stewart and Ken Warner

photo by Mark Hemry at the Fritscher/Hemry home
Sonoma County, September, 2008

End — Clementina Street

2008: photo by Jim Stewart

www.ingramcontent.com/pod-product-compliance
Lightning Source LLC
Chambersburg PA
CBHW031231210726
48287CB00003B/735

* 9 7 8 1 8 9 0 8 3 4 0 3 6 *